Florya Chronicles
of
Political Economy

ISTANBUL AYDIN UNIVERSITY
Journal of Faculty of Economics and Administrative Sciences

Year 4 Number 1 - April 2018

Florya Chronicles of Political Economy

ISSN : 2149-5750

Proprietor
Dr. Mustafa AYDIN

Editor-in-Chief
Zeynep AKYAR

Editor
Prof. Dr. Sedat AYBAR

Editorial Board
Prof. Dr. Sedat AYBAR
Assist. Prof. Dr. Özüm Sezin Uzun

Publication Period
Published twice a year
October and April

Language
English - Turkish

Academic Studies Coordination Office (ASCO)

Administrative Coordinator
Gamze AYDIN

Proofreading
Çiğdem TAŞ

Graphic Desing
Elif HAMAMCI

Visual Design
Nabi SARIBAŞ

Correspondence Address
Beşyol Mahallesi, İnönü Caddesi, No: 38 Sefaköy, 34295 Küçükçekmece/İstanbul
Tel: 0212 4441428
Fax: 0212 425 57 97
Web: www.aydin.edu.tr
E-mail: floryachronicles@aydin.edu.tr

Printed by
Printed by - Baskı
Armoninuans Matbaa
Yukarıdudullu, Bostancı Yolu Cad. Keyap Çarşı B-1 Blk. No: 24
Ümraniye / İSTANBUL
Tel: 0216 540 36 11
Fax: 0216 540 42 72
E-mail: info@armoninuans.com

Scientific Board

Journal of Economic, Administrative and Political Studies is a double-blind peer-reviewed journal which provides a platform for publication of original scientific research and applied practice studies. Positioned as a vehicle for academics and practitioners to share field research, the journal aims to appeal to both researchers and academicians.

ABOUT THE JOURNAL

The Florya Chronicles Journal is the scholarly publication of the İstanbul Aydın University, Faculty of Economics and Administrative Sciences. The Journal is distributed on a twice a year basis. The Florya Chronicles Journal is a peer-reviewed in the area of economics, international relations, management and political studies and is published in both Turkish and English languages. Language support for Turkish translation is given to those manuscripts received in English and accepted for publication. The content of the Journal covers all aspects of economics and social sciences including but not limited to mainstream to heterodox approaches. The Journal aims to meet the needs of the public and private sector employees, specialists, academics, and research scholars of economics and social sciences as well as undergraduate and postgraduate level students. The Florya Chronicles offers a wide spectrum of publication including

- *Research Articles*
- *Case Reports that adds value to empirical and policy oriented techniques, and topics on management*
- *Opinions on areas of relevance*
- *Reviews that comprehensively and systematically covers a specific aspect of economics and social sciences.*

Table of Contents

From the Editor

In this issue of Florya Chronicles, we are presenting you very strong articles on a variety of topics. This is probably due to the `spirit of time` that dictates interdisciplinary work using multilayered methodologies. Although the subject matter of each article varies, a careful reader will notice that these articles share an overriding principle approach that lends support and strengthen political economy framework of inquiry.

The first article by Caşın and Biçer focuses on the security dimension of power politics in the Middle East. They mainly address the rivalries that emerged from confrontations with ISIS that marked the major security concern in the region. They highlight the period starting from 2016, particularly after the intervention of Turkish Armed Forces into the Syrian territory against ISIS and the beginning of the re-organization of the Iraqi Army under American advisors, that reduced the strong position of ISIS in both Syria and Iraq, which in turn has also opened a new stage of international power game. This article makes use of political economy framework in order to develop a detailed analysis of security and what it means for regional rivalries in the long run. Both authors of this important article have day to day, hands on experience on the topic.

The second article shifts attention to a rather different but equally important contemporary development. This is Brexit; the possible exit of Great Britain from the European Union. Now what makes this particular article more interesting is the emphasis it puts upon the impact of Brexit on the Romanian banking sector. The article argues that British Banking system has a relatively special status within the EU banking system, and within this context, one cannot ignore the effects of Brexit on the European financial system and thus on the Romanian banking system. This is also important with regards to the future developments, whereby the process of adopting the euro in Romania will inevitably lead to some changes there. The article discusses that such a development can only be understood behind a backdrop of new arrangements after Brexit, as certain mechanisms within the EU financial and banking system will also change. This article starts by claiming that adoption of a single currency by all member states is the most important aspect of financial integration and integration can never be seen as complete without the adoption of the single European currency at the European institutional level. The issue of single currency has become more and more prevalent. In this regard, the article focuses on the possible effects of Brexit since such a development will have an impact on foreign currency loans market. This is also seen as an important aspect of the evolution of the interbank foreign exchange market that leads to volatility in the interest rates policy part of monetary policy, both at the ECB level and at the Romanian Central Bank level.

The third article turns to a very interesting and more recent topic that has been rather neglected within the political economy milieu, Indian progress in manufacturing that turned the country into a giant industrial hub. This article by Dr. Lalita Som looks at the progress that India has made since 2015, since the launch of the Make in India initiative by the President Modi's government. The article questions whether economic reforms have strengthened the country's manufacturing ecosystem sufficiently to make it a viable global manufacturing hub. Dr. Som uses Kaldorian perspective that examines the relationship between industrial development and economic growth, and bases empirical results characterized the manufacturing sector as "the main engine of fast growth". According to Dr. Som, since the industrial revolution, almost all countries that have managed the transition from low to high income have undergone industrialization, diversifying and upgrading their production structure, reducing their dependence on agriculture and natural resources. As such, using this type of approach one can explain the channels through which manufacturing growth affects economic growth and employment. For Som, this is essential for the way Make in India mobilizes higher labor absorption and leads to better economic outcomes.

The last article by Aybar and Gürel examines the motivations and determinants of China's Outward Foreign Direct Investments (OFDI). The main focus of that article is on the OFDI within the context of The Belt and Road Initiative (BRI) inspired by the ancient Silk Road. Although China's OFDI has always been an important academic interest, BRI initiated OFDI is a distinctive area of study since it is informed by a distinct economic policy that links China to the global set-up. The existing literature on China's OFDI predominantly places its relevant economic policy to the modernization of its national space. What makes China's multivariate domestic economic policy different is that it requires a variety of strategies with diversified outward investments along the BRI route to provide positive returns. The findings in this study indicates that China's OFDI has different motivations ranging from seeking markets, natural resources, establishing strategic assets and efficiency. China aligning its BRI informed investments with its domestic economy aims to *obtain cost advantage, reform its institutions, enlarge market size, establish cultural proximity and sign free trade agreements (FTA). Such alignment and expansion of trade relations with low and middle income countries and their qualified labor force is expected to increase China's global competitiveness. One extra area relates to climate change and global warming. China is accused of being the main global polluter due to its high economic growth rates and industrialization, and aims to reduce CO_2 emissions. This requires a selective industrial policy which affects its OFDI. Besides these, reforming China's state-owned enterprises by broadening their ownership within the BRI led OFDI efforts is expected to increase managerial competitiveness of Chinese enterprises.*

Finally, as per usual, putting together a journal is a collective effort. We have inadvertently received help from our assistants at the Faculty of Economics and Administrative Sciences. We also thank Prof. Celal Nazım Irem, the Dean of the Faculty for his continuous and tireless support to the Florya Chronicles. Our thanks also go to the Rector of Istanbul Aydın University, Prof. Dr. Yadigar İzmirli and our President of Board of Directors, Dr. Mustafa Aydın, whose vision and endless energy for higher achievement in academic excellence has always been an inspiration for us.

Prof. Dr. Sedat Aybar
Editor

Rise and Fall of Isis – Islamic State of Iraq and Syria (Isis) Terrorist Organization; An International Contagious Virus in the New World Order?

R. S. Savaş BIÇER*
Mesut Hakkı CAŞIN**

Abstract

From 2013 until the winter of 2016, ISIS has been in confrontation with Iraqi, Syrian, and Turkish security forces, rival Free Syrian Army, Kurdish Peshmerga fighters, as well as Russian, Iranian and United States led Coalition forces. The group's skill was confirmed by the seizure of crucial provinces in Syria and the quick collapse of Iraqi forces in Mosul and elsewhere in northern Iraq, under the determined assault of outnumbered fighters in the years 2014 and the beginning of 2015. ISIS's clearance of the Sunni areas of the central Iraq to the west and north of Baghdad and the threat to the Kurdish regional areas alarmed the governments across the whole Middle East and the Western powers, particularly in 2015, and during that period, it is generally feared that Saudi Arabia and Jordan might be the next ISIS targets. However, in the year 2016, the strong position of ISIS has declined in both Syria and Iraq particularly immediately after the intervention of Turkish Armed Forces to the Syrian territory against ISIS and the re-organization of the Iraqi Army under the consultancy of United States advisors.

In Middle East, ISIS marks a new threat to the regional security order, at a time of Arab Spring uprisings within the Arab societies and creeping sectarianism fueled mainly by the geostrategic rivalry between Shia and Sunni states of the region. ISIS not only threatens the survival of the people from autocratic regimes, but also the stability of neighboring countries. For military events on the ground to go beyond progress in resolving conflicts and addressing problems of which ISIS is a symptom would not form a

*R.S. Savas Bicer, Assistant Professor at Istanbul Nisantasi University,
** Mesut Hakki Casin, Prof. Dr. at Istanbul İstinye University.

development as far as international security is concerned. To the extent that events in Syria and Iraq do have something to do with a threat of terrorism in the West, that threat will depend not so much on how quickly ISIS expires but rather on what is left after its expiration. Adapting to the new peaceful environment and solving Iraq and Syria problems by mutual understanding will empower the regional countries to limit the spread of this condition. Failure to do so will not only result in a durable threat from ISIS to the region as well as the western counties, but also flowing threats that rise because of continuing challenges to state structures in the Middle East and human security to the democracies in the West.[1]

Keywords: *Terror, security, war, stability, violence, Salafism*

INTRODUCTION

Security may be described as freedom from such phenomena as threat, danger, vulnerability, menace, force and attack.[2] According to the studies about the international terror and security, there are many forms of security, of which international security, national security and human security are the most significantly known, and that the exact meaning of security as such and for each subtype is not only developing but continuously contested as well. It is also suggested by academic environment that the classic civil human rights, in fact, accept four different concepts of security: international security; negative individual security against the state; security as justification to limit human rights; and positive state obligation to offer security to individuals against other individuals.[3] Most important notion that must be focused on is radical Islamism on terrorist attacks. In the following parts of this paper, the features of this type of new security threats will be deeply examined. Terrorism can be accepted as the most significant threat to all kinds of security in these days, especially after the 9/11 attacks committed against the United States (US). Even though the notion of terrorism became so popular and so disputable in the recent years, the roots of terrorism can be traced back to the Scarii Zealots, who were the assassins under the Roman law in the 1st Century AD. With the French Revolution, the meaning of this term became equal to fear, during the administration of Jacobins. The time of anarchism was tried to be

---

[1] Jessica Lewis Mcfate, The Isis Defense in Iraq and Syria: Countering an Adaptive Enemy, *Institute for the Study of War Middle East Security Report 27, May 2015*, p.33

[2] Van Kempen, Piet Hein; "Four Concepts of Security; Human Rights Perspective", *Human Rights Law Review 13- 1 (2013), Oxford University Press, 4 February 2013*, pp.1-23

[3] Van Kempen, 1

suppressed by the actions of the Jacobins to compel the opponent groups by guillotine executions. The French Revolution also introduced the term "terror" to our vocabulary. Most terrorist organizations have understood revolution as secession or national self-determination. This principle, that a people should govern itself, has originated from and protected by the American and French Revolutions. This period initiates the modern notion of terrorist movements generating violent actions to threat the governmental organizations and civilian lives for their political purposes. The modern type of terrorist organizations does not hesitate to obtain heavy arms and harm civilians in mass attacks. The modern terrorism notions have different waves that are affected from the global changes and through these changes, terrorist organizations alter their strategies to realize their aims against authorities.

Right now, as defined in The Four Waves of Rebel Terror and September 11 by David C. Rapoport there are 4 specific phenomena affecting the norms and the actions of terrorist organizations. The first wave covers the years from 1880 to 1914 – until the years of World War I – which is the age of anarcho-terrorism. The second wave is considered to take place from 1919 to 1998. The breakdown of the multinational empires and consequently the post-colonial period of independence caused the ethno-centric terrorist movements. In that period, the Irish Republican Army (IRA), Euskadi Ta Askatasuna (ETA) in Basque region and PKK in Turkey can be the examples of the ethnic terrorism. In the third wave, new-leftist ideology became the trigger of the new terrorist approach. Through the new attitudes in terrorist movements, many of them adapted many ideologies together. Like PKK, many of the ethno-centric terrorist movements express themselves to be Marxist, Leninist, Stalinist or Maoist to collect international support in a bipolar world led by the Cold War. However, the fourth wave of the terrorist approaches caused one of the bloodiest violations in the history, which is the religio-centric terrorism. Al Qaeda, Taliban and the Islamic State of Iraq and Sham (ISIS) induced many historical actions which were resulted in global range migrations and thousands of civilian deaths. The fourth wave have led to the international security politics after the 9/11 attacks to Twin Towers, which was the first foreign terrorist act in the US soil. After this attack caused many civilian deaths, the US has started Global War on Terror, which was the hunting of the members of the Radical Islamist terrorist organizations that were the establishments which accept and declare the US and Israel as their eternal enemies with their Western enemies. This international counter attack to radical ideas of Al Qaeda, opened the way of more radicalized armed groups after specific regional conflicts, like the Iran-Iraq War and the Gulf Wars. All these problems given above bring a question in mind. When the effect of the radical Islamist groups is regarded in Western World through their recruitment systems, can it be said that the religious terrorist organizations, like ISIS, are the new plague for World history?

The waves of the new terrorist attacks in Paris, France, Belgium Airport, Ataturk Airport and lately Istanbul Night Club attack during the early hours of the year 2017 in Turkey, led the international community to focus, again, on the emerging threat against their way of living generated by the Islamic State of Iraq and Syria (ISIS). Indeed, regarding the ISIS case, from beginning to nowadays, it is clearly seen that the terror group was described as the cause of all the above mentioned phenomena and fit into all forms of security listed in previous paragraph.[4] Moreover, the acts of ISIS match the definition of security that can be used and is being used as a political, sometimes even an ideological instrument to govern and reorder society.[5] Today's ISIS's black flag has been raised in a dozen countries outside of Syria and Iraq. The self-proclaimed caliph demands the obedience of all Muslims worldwide. The ISIS claims affiliates in Libya, Egypt, Saudi Arabia, Yemen, Algeria, Afghanistan, Pakistan, Nigeria, Tunisia, the North Caucasus, and terrorist attacks have been carried out in the West, including the United States. Although there are some doubts regarding the authenticity of these claims and the seriousness of the threat that the Islamic State's brand of jihad will spread on a global scale, it is a widely agreed reality that the terrorist organization still is a source of threat, danger, vulnerability, menace, force and attack to the

---

[4] The Soviet defeat and subsequent withdrawal from Afghanistan in 1989 left victorious Arab mujahideen adrift. Many retired from their jihadi adventures returning home to North Africa and the Middle East. Others remained in Pakistan, committed to fighting jihads in other theaters, establishing a network that in 1991 would officially become known as al Qaeda. With time, Osama Bin Laden aimed al Qaeda's ideology at the United States whom he believed to be the 'Far Enemy' who propped up the 'Near Enemy'–local apostate Muslim dictators and their regimes. Al Qaeda and ISIS operate in several contexts: global Salafism, intra-jihadi strife, Sunni alienation from and armed opposition to Shi'a-dominated governments in Baghdad and Damascus, the Arab-Persian conflict, Sunni Arab monarchies, sectarian conflict, and the war against the West. These contexts continually interact with one another. See, Frederick W. Kagan, Kimberly Kagan, Jennifer Cafarella, Harleen Gambhir, and Katherine Zimmerman: "U.S. Grand Strategy: Destroying ISIS and al Qaeda, Report One- Al Qaeda and ISIS: Existential Threats to the U.S and Europe", ISW –Institute for the Study of War, January 2016, http://www.understandingwar.org/sites/default/files/PLANEX%20Report%201%20--%20FINALFINALFINAL.pdf.
[5] Neocleous Mark, "Critique of Security", *Edinburgh University Press 2008*, pp 4-5.

international security, national security and human security ever seen as far as religious basement is concerned. In this context, rather than other terrorist organizations, ISIS is a dangerous threat that attacks not only individual security, but also national and international security.[6]

1. A THEORETICAL EXPLANATION: UNDERSTANDING COMPLEX NATURE OF RELIGION AND TERRORISM

Terrorism is certainly a form of political violence caused coordinated destruction, but this is not the only definition for terrorism, there are also other collective events, such as race riots, some protest events, or violent encounters between rulers and their subjects. There can be several questions to understand the theoretical framework of terrorism in the light of this definition. After Cold War, changing ideology initiatives produced a different motivation or rhetoric. There is a surprisingly wide range of religious terrorism threats; the coming of a fifth wave must stand in line with all sorts of other criminal violence and overtaken secular leftist or radical ethnic separatism that become the main driver of terrorist attacks on global sphere. This indicates terrorism is not only served as political violence, it can also rely on religious, ideological, nationalist, ethnic or personal goals, and terrorists may be personally motivated by a sense of humiliation, perceived injustice, or socioeconomic deprivation. Indeed, according to Global Terrorism Index, religious extremism has become the main driver of terrorism in modern world.[7] For that reason, it should be asked why religiously motivated terrorism is becoming more common and why new religious terrorism waves are more deadly. To clarify the point, the fundamental ideologies leading the religious terrorism in the modern world must be considered in order to grasp the impacts on religious terrorism. In parallel with that, Richard T. Antoun states that "the religious orientation views religion as relevant to all important domains of culture and society."[8] Moreover, Steve Bruce divides fundamentalism into two distinct types: firstly, communal (giving Middle-Eastern Islam as an example); secondly, individual (giving strict Protestant conservatives

---

[6] Lewis Jessica D., "The Islamic State: a Counter-Strategy for a Counter-State", *Institute for the Study of War, Middle East Security Report 21, July 2014*, pp.2-4

[7] The report recorded 18,000 deaths in 2013, a rise of 60% on the previous year. The majority (66%) of these were attributable to just four groups: Islamic State in Iraq and Syria (ISIS), Boko Haram in Nigeria, the Taliban in Afghanistan and al-Qaida. "Religious extremism is the main cause of terrorism, according to report", The Guardian, 18 October 2014, https://www.theguardian.com/news/datablog/2014/nov/18/religious-extremism-main-cause-of-terrorism-according-to-report,

[8] Antoun (2001) p2.

as an example).[9] In order to analyze today's greatest problem, which is
extremist religious terrorism in global range, in first hand, one must focus
on the theory of the religious extremism that cause terrorism by several
actors such as; Al Qaeda and ISIS. For understanding religious extremism
that cause terrorism, we must understand the fundamentalist approach to
religion.

Fundamentalism, in a basic sense, is a reaction against modernity and there
are also other aspects of the concept adopted by its followers. To analyze
the Al Qaeda and ISIS as a religious extremist movement, fundamentalism
alone is not enough to explain the aspects of these groups. As a result,
our focus moves on Islamic Religious Fundamentalism and its features.
Anti-modernity is the most intensive characteristics of fundamentalism
that is a type of a religious framework evolved to defend religion in front
of the modern world necessities. Thus, the rejection of the modern world
means to be against the Western world and their innovations (Toft et
al., 2011). In addition to this definition in God's Century, sociologist of
religion David Lehman describes "fundamentalist religious globalization"
as the way fundamentalists establish themselves a new culture "without
acknowledging this new culture."[10] The anti-modernity aspect of religious
fundamentalism brings the understanding of myth of the Golden Age. The
Golden Age of the religion indicates where religion is pure and perfect
according to their subjects. However, the Golden Age, as a period, can
differ from one interpretation of religion to another. The religion of Islam
is one of the obvious examples for the variability in the explanation of the
Qur'an. The goal of the religious fundamentalist ideology is its relationship
to religious texts. According to them, the holy texts are fundamental,
essential and authentic. They are considered the inherent and infallible
sources for religious authenticity and are to be taken literally. Today, there
are two popular explanations among the devoted people of the religious
fundamental groups, which are Wahhabi and Salafi movement. Regarding
the religious terrorism in 21st century, Al Qaeda and the ISIS are two
important Salafist groups of the fundamentalist. In the light of this, these
two terrorist groups' followers believe the Golden Age of Islam to be the

---

[9] Bruce (2008) chapter 1, page 8-9. Chapter 3 of his book covers the communal form, and chapter four covers
the individual kind.
[10] Lehman, David (2002). "Religion and Globalization". In Linda Woodhead, Paul Fletcher, Hiroko Kawanami,
and David Smith (eds.), Religion in the Modern World: Traditions and Transformations. London: Routledge,
299-315. Sourced from "Migration and the Globalization of Religion" by Caroline Plüss (2011) p493-4, 498.

term of the Prophet Mohammed (Peace be Upon Him) and his Caliphates. There was an absence of distinction between public and private spheres during that period. Also, there was hierarchical and patriarchal relationship between genders at the time, which indicates the public in male domination. According to literal interpretation of Qur'an, the Salafists must meet the Golden Age's way of life. There are some restrictions in member's daily life in Salafi movement. The members who are selected by special recruitment procedure generally pursue specific dress codes or rhetoric derived from the Prophet's time (PBUH).

The affiliation in the religious fundamental groups starts with an election among the members, and those members are expected to espouse the requirements of this group, immediately after being chosen. The examination of group psychology may be more helpful toward understanding the role of religious factors together with other factors in fundamental ideology and religious terrorist violence. In his article "The role of religious fundamentalism in terrorist violence: A social psychological analysis", M. Brooke Rogers says "A discussion of terrorist group dynamics cannot take place without first grounding the group interactions in the social psychology of ethnocentrism and intergroup conflict." The religious fundamentalist groups keep their minds straight and dedicated. The controversies are clear in their understandings, the relation between right and wrong, good and evil or salvation and damnation are accrued. For that reason, the difference between the Western world and themselves has sharp edges. According to the Islamic thought adopted by these fundamental groups, the Western world is the sinner. To control this depravation of the Western world, the belief of Jihadism is very common among the Islamic religious fundamental groups. Former Egyptian Muslim Brotherhood ideologue Sayyid Qutb states that offensive jihad is a radical belief that can be traced to the dark cells., Egypt's concentration camps of the Nasser Era can be accepted as a birth place of offensive jihad. Qutb was also one of the residents of this camp and he was one of the original theorists of modern Islamism by defining his radical thoughts. Due to Jihadist comprehension in Islamic world, there are two different types of Jihad explication to fight with infidels who live in the Western world; the first, The Little Jihad that includes the fight with sword. According to Islamic Doctrine, the physical jihad (The Little Jihad) refers to a defensive measure to be permitted only during acts of aggression upon the Muslim Community (Ummah).

Additionally, The Great Jihad that aims to conquer the corrupted minds with the philosophy of Islam. However, to Qutb, jihad was not simply a tool limited to the defensive struggle against external aggression nor was it restricted to the spiritual jihad (inner struggle).

Rather, he consigned the physical jihad to an illimitable utilitarian contrivance to be employed for an offensive assault in order to reform societies by spreading Islam, and to liberate all men, both Muslim and non-Muslim. Beyond the Cold War era in the world politics terrorist attacks tactics, reflecting new symptoms that are identical to the transformation conflicts nature, there has been a rise in the proportion of terrorists motivated by religious concerns, and there is a significant correlation between religious motivation and lethality. Indeed, the ongoing new terrorist violence that concerns the international community is mostly religion based and motivated by "sacred values". Also, destructive attack methods such as suicide bombing, martyrdom and the use of weapons are symbolic features of religion based terrorism. Furthermore, members of terrorist organizations expressing dissatisfaction in nation-state politics in the name of religion aim at realizing their ideologies in parallel to political motives. Such as ISIS misreading Western Democracies for being unfair and weak. They assume their ideologies and principles are just, stronger, determined, and powerful and the God will assists from its side perspectives. Except their way, all other political systems which do not have sufficient faith in God, will basically become out of heart in terms of human civilization.

2. THE INFLUENCE OF ISID IN THE MIDDLE EAST REGION

Understanding salafism has a crucial importance in the explanation of the influence of ISIS in Middle East region. Salafism, paradoxically, as an apolitical ideology, has become a major force in the world politics, beginning with the Arab Spring that started in January, 2011. This movement also marked a significant turn regarding the Islamism in the twentieth century. The events of the Arab Spring have led to new political realities in the Arab world and paved the way for the ISIS to form a so-called state on the soils of Iraq and Syria. It is encouraged by "Arab Spring" movements, like the Muslim Brotherhood in Jordan and Egypt; ISIS played a leading role in the Sunni uprising after the operation of US led coalition in Iraq at the beginning. The ISIS movement today is in open confrontation with the Iraq and Syria regime, and suffers from external intervention. The disastrous outcome of the Arab Spring for Syria, Libya, and Yemen as well as the banning of the Muslim Brotherhood in Egypt, Saudi Arabia, and the United Arab Emirates (UAE) have strengthened the movement's influence in the region, especially in Syria. Its political future in Iraq now depends on government's decisive acts, but mostly on its ability to solve internal discriminatory politics in the country, although Syria's future depends on the success of the opposition forces excluding ISIS. This article presents a research on the threat of radical groups of warring factions during the Syrian Civil War so far, particularly the rise of ISIS[11] in an academic point of view, and argues that the consequences of the Arab Spring has had a serious positive impact on the ISIS both in Iraq and Syria, moreover, in the region. The outcomes of the research demonstrate that the serious international and regional efforts would be required to diminish not only ISIS's previous military-political role and influence, but also the other terrorist movements in the region.

The impact of 9/11 changing the main governmental regulations and actions that decide to fight against terrorism under the rule of law which is called War on Terror is being universally discussed. One of the main incidents that happened in 1948 is the declaration of Israel's independence, in consequence of which the first Arab- Israel War has erupted. The belligerents of this war, Israel and the Arab League which is a collective force including Egypt, Jordan, Iraq, Syria, and Saudi Arabia, fought in the second stage of 1948 Palestinian War (Tal, 2005). Obviously, the main reasons of this war were the independence declaration of Israel.

The United Nations (UN) General Assembly adopted a proposal which was called UN Partition Plan for Palestine –UN General Assembly Resolution 181 III— was a step for solving the Arab-Jewish problem (United Nations, 1990). This resolution brought a specific condition in the Middle East. After Israel gained its independence, most of the Jews migrated to Israel from all over the world. In contrary, most of the Arab population had to mobilize from the territory that they live in where today happens to be the Israeli territory. Many civilians have died during this process. Moreover, the distribution of oil, as a new resource, started to gain importance in

---

[11] Daesh sounds similar to an Arabic word that means to bruise or crush; the group's leaders consider the word insulting. This article unintentionally uses ISIS rather than "Daesh" to strip away any religious or political legitimacy that the acronym suggests.

the Middle East region and for the whole world. Through the territorial problems in the region, nationalist movements had spread (Peteet, 2005). In a nutshell, first Arab- Israel War resulted with the victory of Israel. However, it was a beginning of an endless crisis in the region.

Suez Crisis is another issue that affected the whole region. Egyptian President Gamal Abdel Nasser declared the nationalization of the Suez Canal Company in 1956; this situation caused a critical tension between Egypt, Britain, and France.[12] Nasser described himself as a representative of the third world countries. When we come to the year of 1967, Six Day War was confronted. When we look at the Six Day War, Syria was a part of this conflict against Israel, and the results were similar to the first Arab-Israeli Wars (Mann, 2013). This war had important results for the Middle East, though; Golan Heights were captured in Syria by the Israeli forces. The importance of the Golan Heights was related to water sources. The conflicts between Israel and Arab world were a longstanding competition. In 1973, The Yom Kippur War arose. This War started with an unexpected Arab attack on Israel on Saturday, the 6th of October.

It can be clearly seen from the historical background of the conflicts; the struggles of the authorities for productive lands lead to instability in Modern Middle East. The Iran-Iraq War was miscellaneous, and it contained religious differentiations, political varieties and border debates. This was the other reason for the inconstancy in the region. Conflicts continued as old Sunni-versus-Shia and Arab-versus-Persian religious and ethnic disputes, and grew to a personal hostility between Saddam Hussein and Ayatollah Khomeini.[13] The Iran-Iraqi War in 1988 was the turning point for the Middle East region, and it demonstrates The Soviet Union and other Western powers seeing Iraq, as the balancer of the newly changed regime of Iran. For that reason, they let Saddam to export weapons into the country. The western powers supplied chemical and biological weapons to Iraq to help Saddam's administration (Bulloch & Morris, 1989)"title" : "The Gulf War: Its Origins, History and Consequences", "type" : "paper-conference"}, "uris" : ["http://www.mendeley.com/documents/?uuid=4caec9a9-043b-4d5d-b129-3ed48d306cd6"] }],"mendeley" : {"formattedCitation": "(Bulloch & Morris, 1989.)

---

[12] https://history.state.gov/milestones/1953-1960/suez
[13] http://www.iranchamber.com/history/iran_iraq_war/iran_iraq_war1.php

However, as it is a well-known fact, the claims on the mass destruction weapons under Saddam's Iraq which was intervened by international collective forces after Saddam had invaded Kuwait, where is a critical point for the Middle Eastern petrol transfers to West, in the early 1990's. The so called humanitarian intervention led to the overthrow of the whole Saddam administration members from Iraq, and such a reduction in the number of bureaucratic people created an extreme authority gap. Saddam was very powerful in controlling the local tribes who belonged to various backgrounds and believes. After he was captured by the US, those people decided to establish a new form of authority which is against leadership. In a roundabout way, this situation helps a movement like ISIS to rise in a very strong way and in a short time. When the actions of ISIS are compared with the system of Taliban and al-Qaeda; ISIS is more lethal, and the recruitment process is more widened. ISIS can attempt to kill many people even the Sunni Muslim civilians, however others follow a path to separate sinner and inner.

3. POLITICAL CONSTRUCTION OF CALIPHATE OR FAIL OF SYKES-PICOT[14]IMPOSITION

Hundreds of Syrians have lost their lives in almost five years of armed conflict, which began with anti-regime ruins before escalating into a full-scale civil war in the year 2011 in Syria as an aftershock of "Arab Spring".[15] The opposition's demands included economic, social and political rights, and the regime not being overthrown caused the catastrophic outcomes in a few years. Millions of people other than the protesters were forced out of their homes, as the forces of President Bashar al-Assad and those opposed to his rule as well as jihadist militants from opposition battle against one another. Below is the chart of the designated current warring factions and the parties of the confrontation in Syria, in the brutal civil war.

---

[14] Syces-Picot Agreement; available online at; http://www.history.com/this-day-in-history/britain-and-france-conclude-sykes-picot-agreement

[15] Joya Angela, "Syria and the Arab Spring: The Role of the Domestic and External Factors", Understanding the Syrian Crisis: Causes, Actors and Outcomes, International Conference "The Arab Spring: Between Authoritarianism and Revolution", March 12-13, Center for the Advanced Study of the Arab World at Durham University, United Kingdom 2012, p.32

Table 1: Messy relations in Syria in the beginning of the conflicts

	ISIS	TUR	US/EU	SDF	IRAN	RUS	FSA	SYR. Gov.
ISIS	-	E	E	E	E	E	E	E
TURKEY	E	-	F	E	N	N/U	F	E
US/EU	E	F	-	F	E	E	N	E
SDF	E	E	F	-	N/M	F	E	E
IRAN	E	N	E	N/M	-	F	E	F
RUSSIA	E	N/U	N	F	F	-	E	F
FSA	E	F	F	E	E	E	-	E
SYR.Gov.	E	E	E	E	F	F	E	-

(F: Friendly, E: Enemy, N: Neutral, U: Unfriendly, M: Mistrust)

Pro-democracy protests rose in the March of 2011 in Syria, following the security forces opening fire on demonstrators and killing several; more protesters took to the streets. Since the major unrest began in March 2011, various reports suggest the number of Syrians that were killed to be between 17,000 and 18,000.[16] The unrest triggered countrywide protests demanding President's resignation. The government's use of force to crush the dissent merely hardened the protesters' resolve. By the mid-summer of 2011, thousands were taking to the streets across the country. Opposition supporters eventually began to take up arms, first to defend themselves and later to expel security forces from their local areas. The regime maintained the use of deadly force against its citizens in continued to violate international human rights and humanitarian law as well as its agreement in November 2011;[17] the Arab League plan to engage in reforms and cease killing civilians.[18]Although for many years prior to 2011, the regime of Syrian President Bashar al-Assad had maintained a consistently flirtatious relationship with Sunni jihadists, under the new circumstances, they have become the most dangerous enemies for each other now. Thus, Damascus can no more aim at manipulating them into acting as proxies for Syria's agenda of regional policy.

---

[16] Sharp Jeremy M.,Christopher M. Blanchard,"Armed Conflict in Syria: U.S. and International Response", Congressional Research Service (CSR) Report for Congress July 2012.
[17] Available online at; http://www.bbc.com/news/world-middle-east-12794882
[18] Syria 2012 Human Rights Report, available online at; https://www.hrw.org/world-report/2012/country-chapters/syria

4. THE FALL OF AL QAEDA, THE RISE OF ISIS

The moment it felt an unfortunate, appropriate international recklessness, the radical jihadi group ISIS has captured Mosul, Iraq's second-largest city; Tikrit, Saddam Hussain's birth city; and many other towns along the way on its fast advance through Iraq.[19] Furthermore, with the help of former Baathists and Sunni tribal forces, the group made its way toward Baghdad. ISIS' astonishing success could be a sign of a structural change within the radical terrorist movement. ISIS assumes the role of Al Qaeda, as the movement's leader. His power struggle and the friction between the two groups is not new. Meanwhile the relationship did not reach a breaking point until April 2013, when ISIS expanded its movement into Syria and attempted to attach the local Al Qaeda branches under its authority.

After multiple failed attempts at mediation by various leading sheikhs in the global jihadist community, the two groups split permanently when the leader of Al-Qaeda central formally repudiated ISIS.[20] Not only Al Qaeda's leader, but also other branch leaders rejected this fait accompli and tried to calm the dispute by announcing that Al Qaeda would remain responsible for jihad in Syria and ISIS would keep to Iraq. ISIS immediately refused to accept this decision and continued its expansion into Syria, trampled other Syrian rebel groups, including radical Islamists. When ISIS' overreach provoked a backlash, opposing rebel groups mounted a counteroffensive and they sided with the anti-ISIS forces. By February 2014, the split between ISIS and the Syrian opposition had led Al Qaeda to disown the group.[21]

The differences between ISIS and Al Qaeda are not just about power and control of the jihadi movement. As important as these features are, the groups have serious differences when it comes to strategy, tactics, and Islamic authority. Their characteristics differ from each other such as the implementation of strict Islamist laws and the understanding of right of one group to enforce its authority over all others. The groups don't disagree about the legitimacy of these things, but Al Qaeda is more tolerant, and ISIS

---

[19] Shaul Shay, "The Threat of The New Caliphate", International Institute for Counter-Terrorism (ICT), August 2014, p.5
[20] Available online at; http://www.thedailybeast.com/articles/2014/02/03/al-qaeda-denounces-syrian-jihadistgroup-isis.html
[21] Hubbard Ben, Al Qaeda Breaks With Jihadist Group in Syria Involved in Rebel Infighting, the New York Times, Feb. 3, 2014, available online at; http://www.nytimes.com/2014/02/04/world/middleeast/syria.html?_r=0

is generally more radical and inflexible. ISIS' display of power, particularly the military successes, brought the group considerable rewards, so ISIS captured huge amounts of military equipment, and liberated hundreds of fighters from prisons in the territory that is now under its control.

Furthermore, ISIS' reputation rises among radicals, and these successes will transform into more money and volunteers for the organization. In this context, ISIS is able to mobilize those forces rapidly along the disappearing border between Iraq and Syria, which it gradually controls more, and organizes even more motivated campaigns in Syria. The terrorist group's march through Iraq also diminishes Al Qaeda's profile while raising ISIS'. ISIS seems to be realizing the reestablishment of the Caliphate, although Al Qaeda has started the march toward same direction thirteen years ago by its greatest achievement which is 9/11 attacks. Al Qaeda controlled territories that were smaller in size and significance than what ISIS controls today.[22]

In accordance with its success, ISIS gained legitimacy and overwhelmed Al Qaeda's main tactic to delegitimize the movement. Until now, Al Qaeda's strategy had been slightly successful, so some jihadi scholars released messages of support for Al Qaeda and strongly condemned ISIS fans. However, all that plays to ISIS' favor since young jihadist give more respect to warriors than to religious scholars. As far as symbolism is concerned, ISIS holds a territory larger than many countries[23] and owning this amount of land works to ISIS' advantage. Unfortunately for Iraqis and Syrians, ISIS' losing its gains seems unlikely to happen. It is unpredicted that the collapsing Iraqi military is which is ill-equipped, to quickly reverse ISIS' progress since it is the result of a well-thought-out plan that was structured for a long time. Additionally, individuals like winners and, unlike Al-Qaeda, which has not had a clear victory in a decade, ISIS continues to build its prestige and legitimacy within the overall movement.[24]

Al-Qaeda knows that ISIS is an extremely capable force whereas its battle achievements do not make it any more appealing as a government. To succeed in the competition with ISIS, Al Qaeda could try to beat it in some

---

[22] Caris Charles C. & Samuel Reynolds, "ISIS Governance in Syria", Institute for the Study of War, Middle East Security Report 22, July 2014, pp.24-25

[23] Cockburn Patrick, "ISIS consolidates", London Review 36, no.16, pp.1-2, August 2014, available online at; http://www.lrb.co.uk/v36/no16/patrich-cockburn/isis-consolidates.

[24] Zelin Aaron Y., "The War between ISIS and al-Qaeda for Supremacy of the Global Jihadist Movement", The Washington Institute for Near East Policy no.20, June 2014, p.7

way such as through advances against the Assad regime, medium scale operations in the Arabian Peninsula and in North Africa, and individual or lone-wolf type terrorist attacks in the western countries. Continued success for ISIS, of course, is by no means guaranteed, especially given the group's tendency to overplay its hand with locals.[25]

5. WHAT DOES SALAFISM WANT?

In the wake of serious terror attacks in addition to the group's statements, social media posts, videos and also the flood of concurring information, ISIS seems bent on confrontation with the West. Although the relationship between the group's strategy, politics, and religious ideology is complex, understanding it is the first step for confronting it in the correct way. Meanwhile, the problem is relatively easy to state, but extremely difficult to solve.[26]Although Salafism is characteristically nonpolitical, leading Salafists criticized political groups, particularly the Muslim Brotherhood for being distracted by modern concerns. Since a definition of Salafism is in order, some Salafists choose to remain outside of the political arena altogether, while others jump right in. Like the ideology of the Muslim Brotherhood, Salafism is often lumped together with Islamism, although they are practically not the same thing. The Muslim Brotherhood seeks to introduce Islam into the political sphere while Salafism is strictly Sunni and discusses an obscure theological concept than any mention of strategy or goals. Although some type of Islamism accommodates the trappings of modern political life, the Salafists' do not. Meanwhile, the Arab Spring saw the formation of Salafist parties participating in post-revolution political transitions by betraying the Salafist principles of rejecting modern institutions. For some Salafist groups, participating in political processes has been a clever strategic choice, keeping them out of their local governments' targeting sights. This choice has opened them not only to the criticism of other political parties but also other Salafist groups, thus this issue has cost them their popular supporters to regard them as betrayers to the principles in favor of their political needs, moreover, this also brings us to the case of ISIS; it openly rejects the political jargon of constitutions and modern politics.

---

[25] Zelin, 6
[26] Kagan Kimberly, Frederick W. Kagan, & Jessica D. Lewis, A Strategy to defeat the Islamic State, Institute for the Study of War, Middle East Security Report 23, September 2014, p.6

> *"Some Salafis violate ideological principles by forming political parties (e.g., Egypt, Gulf States), with some arguing that this is justified as a way of perpetuating their mission of purification and education (al-tasfiya wa-l-tarbiya)."*[27]

ISIS texts, much like those of other Salafists, are filled with discussions of the hadith, early Islamic theological concepts, and statements from specific pre-modern figures thought to uphold the Salafist faith. Nevertheless, ISIS, unlike Al Qaeda, has been able to make its theology applicable to real-world political objections and won recruits by promising true Islam and it seems that it deems military training of secondary importance as compared to the effort that it puts into cultivating the combatants' desire to fight.[28] The terrorist organization dedicates big energy to classroom tools explaining its theological views, and eventually, its success will depend on this dense and concentrated program. Its firm commitment to establishing a theologically faithful state rather than a modern political one makes a trustworthy reputation among its believers. To achieve his educational goals, The Islamic State sometimes appropriates schools and other institutions, giving those working within them the "option" of keeping their positions, but surely under its control and in educational aims of the organization.[29] Although ISIS's territorial expansion in targeted lands and attacks on the Western countries will continue to attract local populations and adherents, those are not the only reasons for its successes.

The group's doctrinally consistent bypassing of Western political culture has allowed it to gain so many recruits. The ISIS' attacks to the West created a broad international consensus that the terrorist organization is on the march and must be stopped. The United States had announced as much in September 2014 that the United States would seek to "degrade and ultimately destroy" the group, but cautioned that the campaign would be long and difficult. Washington settled on a gradual approach that involved a very limited application of force rather than to commit ground forces. In fact, this slow strategy had given ISIS time to combine its control, train terrorists, and set in operatives in the region. Under these suitable

---

[27] Olidort Jacob, "Salafism: Ideas, Recent History, Politics ",Available online at; http://www. washingtoninstitute.org/uploads/Documents/other/Salafism-Olidort-2.pdf

[28] Siboni Gabi, "The Military Power of the Islamic State", The Institute for National Security Studies, January 2015, p.65

[29] Khatib Lina, "The Islamic State's Strategy: Lasting and Expanding", Carnegie Middle East Center, June 2014, p.7

circumstances, unlike Al Qaeda, which does not directly manage the daily operations of its franchises, ISIS claims to have direct control over the fighters and residents in its territory, thus applies a new type of less flexible and hierarchical structure.

Also, winning the territorial battle would deprive ISIS of important practical and propaganda advantages such as the taxes and other resources available to ISIS because it controls territory and a civilian population will be gone. The idea that ISIS victories are ordained by God and that therefore Muslims should join it will be undermined.[30] The most recent message by Al-Qaeda leadership on beginning of the year 2017 marks a new escalation between the two rival groups, and attacks ISIS leadership strongly.[31] It coincides with military operations against ISIS in Iraq and Syria, which have, to some degree, cut back the group's human and financial resources. Meanwhile, Al-Qaeda is striving, once again, to become the top terrorist organization in the world after declining on the organizational and operational levels.

6. UNITED STATES AND ITS RESPONSE TO ISIS THREAT

The United States' bitter experiences in Iraq and Afghanistan shaped its initial response to ISIS. However, after the entrance of ISIS to the regional Picture, "Containment of the Violence Policy" of the US administration was changed, and it was understood that strategy was no longer valid. Rather than the strategy of staying away from Middle Eastern conflicts, a gradual increasing in US involvement in Iraq and expanding the U.S. bombing campaign to Syria was preferred by Washington. The main problem of defeating ISIS commitment was the need for ground forces, which the United States has been reluctant to provide. Instead of direct application of U.S. power, empowering allies to assume a greater share of the burden strategy has worked well.

The US support for the Kurdish people is only valid for the Kurds who lives in Syria. To be clearer, as we all are familiar, after 9/11 USA have sent troops to Afghanistan and Iraq, and when Obama came to power, he promised that all the US soldiers will be withdrawn from Afghanistan and

---

[30] Smith Ben, Claire Mills, "Syria and Iraq: update July 2017", Briefing Paper Number CBP 8011, House of Common Library, 21 July 2017, p.28
[31] Available online at; http://english.aawsat.com/2017/01/article55365124/zawahiri-strongly-criticizes-baghdadi, accessed on; 09 January 2017

Iraq. As a democrat president, he made this promise. In the process between 2012 and 2016, the USA did not exist in Middle East territories physically. In parallel with this, Obama created cooperation between Kurds and the US in order to protect its own interests in the Syrian issue.

What is the US aim towards Syria? This question is also important to understand why the USA supports Kurds in the Syria region. Basically, we can say that, the prime purpose of the US is to prevent establishment of a radical religious state in Syria. The US is the archenemy of the radical religious groups. The US has always two types of plans on the foreign policy, the long term plan and the short-term plan. Supporting Kurds on Syria is the short-term plan of the US. Another important point that is related with the US and ISIS is the US government seeing PYD and YPG as important forces in front of ISIS. Although there are immense contradictions which all came from Turkish authorities, the US found the Kurdish forces in Iraq and Syria to be reliable and highly capable allies. According to US, Kurdish forces courageously blocked ISIS's advance and recaptured most of the ISIS occupied areas in Iraq and Syria including so-called ISIS capital city Raqqa, thus cutting all lines of communications of terrorists. However, rather than Iraq Kurdish Peshmerga forces, Syrian Kurdish rebel YPG[32] which is an extension of PKK terrorist organization, is seen as a friendly force even for the US, since they are engaged in fighting the ISIS.[33]

The above mentioned optimistic approach is not valid in ISIS-controlled territory. Sunni Arabs who object to ISIS are likely to fear Kurdish expansionism and may join hands with ISIS to resist their advance, since Kurdish victories in the Arab territories have already been met with accusations that the Kurds are trying to expand their control at the expense of the locals. Therefore, sectarian apprehension would make relying on Shia forces in Iraq to capture ISIS occupied lands even more challenging. It is clear that the Shia-dominated regime in Iraq is not going to surrender control to allow an American–Sunni partnership and insist that any support

---

[32] The Democratic Union Party (Partiya Yekîtiya Demokrat, PYD) is a Kurdish faction, founded in 2003. PYD is ideologically, organizationally and militarily, affiliated with the PKK terrorist organization. The People's Defense Corps (Yekîneyên Parastina Gel, YPG) is the PYD's armed branch.

[33] Hassan Hassan," Unconditional U.S. Support for Kurdish Forces in Syria Harms the Anti-ISIS Cause", The New York Times, 24 February 2016, available online at; http://www.nytimes.com/roomfordebate/2016/02/24/are-kurds-allies-or-obstacles-in-syria/unconditional-us-support-for-kurdish-forces-in-syria-harms-the-anti-isis-cause

to the Sunnis must be passing through the central government.[34] So far the conditions are not different in Syria, and Sunni Arabs view Assad's regime as dangerous and threatening as ISIS. Although anti-PYD sources claim that the PYD staged uprisings in coordination with the regime and alleged that regime had handed over five provinces to the PYD, the gains of PYD in previously Sunni-majority areas are mostly appreciated by Syrian Sunni population.[35] It is actually true that the PYD's enhanced control in the north arguably presented potential benefits for the regime, and forced other armed opposition groups, obstructing their access to border areas by raising the movement's profile, and worsened fears among many Syrians as well. In the end, and regardless of whether the regime and PYD might have cooperated and to what extent, the PYD secured several areas of the north, while the regime took no action to recover them.[36] United States' resistance to the pressures to escalate its involvement in conflicts against regime forces caused failure of the "train and equip" program of US[37] and Turkey.[38] The few individuals that enrolled in the program were killed or forced to surrender their weapons.

When it was widely accepted that the ISIS threat is too urgent to simply wait for the proto-state to collapse from within after the Paris attacks, US strategy was modified. It is seen that the slow progress in Iraq and Syria only increases the threat of terrorism abroad. Although members of the international community can be expected to strengthen their ability to stop terrorist threats through more robust internal security and better international cooperation, U.S. recognized that ever-greater burden sharing cannot substitute for its deeper involvement. The key to dealing with the threat is to quickly and effectively face ISIS in its strongholds in the Middle East. Contrary to the expectations of some politicians and political thinkers[39], previous U.S. strategy did not cover direct military intervention,

---

[34] Hinnebusch Raymond, "The American Invasion of Iraq: Causes and Consequences", Perceptions Spring 2007, p.19

[35] US Defense Secretary Ash Carter's testimony to the Senate Armed Services Committee, December 9, 2015, available online at; http://www.defense.gov/News-Article-View/Article/633554/carter-says-isil-must-be-defeated-in-its-parent-tumor?source=GovDelivery

[36] International Crisis Group, "Syria's Kurds: A Struggle Within a Struggle", Middle East Report N°136, Brussels, 22 January 2013,pp.15-16

[37] Blanchard Christopher M., Amy Belasco, "Train and Equip Program for Syria: Authorities, Funding, and Issues for Congress", Congressional Research Service Report, June 9, 2015, pp.1-2

[38] Byman Daniel, "Six Bad Options for Syria", The Washington Quarterly, Winter 2016, p.171

[39] Kagan Kimberly, "U.S. Role and Strategy in the Middle East: Syria, Iraq, and the Fight Against ISIS", statement before the Senate Committee on Foreign Relations September 16, 2015, pp.2-4

and "Enabling local forces -- not substituting for them -- is necessary to ensure a lasting defeat of ISIL" was declared as a new strategy.[40]

The new U.S. administration primarily needs to rethink key aspects of the struggle against not only the Islamic extremism, but also all types of terrorism itself. U.S. and Western partners need to see it as a continuing threat that will be present for, at least, the coming decade, regardless of what happens to ISIS. They also need to consider how this threat is tied to the confrontation between Iran and most Arab states, and the growing tensions between Sunnis and Shi'ites. They need to stop thinking largely in terms of terrorism and consider the threat posed in terms of insurgency and efforts to seize control of largely Muslim states. They also need to address the fact that any strategy based on counterterrorism alone will fail unless they also cooperate in addressing the causes of terrorism, insurgency, and unrest.[41]

7. RUSSIAN POLITICS AND SYRIA INTERVENTION WITH TARGETING ISIS

After the collapse of USSR, as a newly emerged system, Russia adopted some basic strategies for its foreign affairs in a very similar way that existed before. After the Arab Spring movements and the civil war in Syria, Russia tends to collaborate with Iran and China which were allies for a long time. One must bear in mind that, today, Putin's Russia plays a key role on the Syrian Civil war. Furthermore, it helps Turkey to fight with ISIS in parallel with Euphrates Shield Operation as an indirect way with the aircraft bombings. Following its general support for the hard-pressed Assad regime, Russia moved to establish a small task force in regime-controlled territory near the north-west city of Latakia in September 2015, and then started attacks using strike aircraft and helicopter gunships at the end of the month[42]. Firstly, according to the Russian leadership, the move reconfirmed Russia's status as a crucial power, and secondly broke down its international isolation by diverting attention from Ukraine. Also, United States softened its position on Syrian President Bashar al-Assad,

---

[40] US Defense Secretary Ash Carter's testimony to the Senate Armed Services Committee, Washington, April 28, 2016, available online at; http://www.defense.gov/News/Speeches/Speech-View/Article/744936/statement-on-counter-isil-operations-and-us-military-strategy-in-the-middle-east

[41] Anthony H. Cordesman, "Rethinking the Threat of Islamic Extremism: The Changes Needed in U.S. Strategy", *Center for International Strategic Studies, January 3, 2017*, p.2

[42] Rogers Paul, Richard Reeve," Russia's Intervention in Syria: Implications for Western Engagement", Oxford Research Group Global Security Briefing, October 2015, p.2

whose resignation is no longer considered a precondition for settlement. Most importantly, winning some applause in the EU may create conditions for sanctions relief.[43]

In the beginning, Russia mounted an intensive information campaign to highlight the significance of what it was doing. Later, it gradually accelerated the degree of intervention and initially used relatively old aircrafts and unguided bombs. Russia added to these efforts by firing cruise missiles from warships in the Caspian Sea which overflew Iran and Iraq with the agreement of these governments, even if to be resulting with the deaths and injuries of civilians.[44]

Most of the Russian air strikes have been against the forces opposed to the Assad regime rather than IS, and indeed, IS used the opportunity to make gains on the ground against anti-Assad forces pre-occupied with fighting Syrian Army units.[45] One of the reasons of the Russian operations timing can be considered as an easing of the intensity of the conflict in eastern Ukraine, and assist to emphasize Putin's firmness that Russia is still a great power beyond its near environment. Bearing all these factors in mind, Putin, of course, fears IS' advance however, less than he fears the collapse of the Assad regime.

Russia's direct involvement in the war in Syria is not likely to secure anything more than tactical or localized victory for the Assad regime. Therefore, it is a fact that Russian military operations in Syria did not directly affect ISIS since they did not directly aim ISIS. On 14 March 2016, Russian President Vladimir Putin surprised the world with an announcement of the withdrawal of Russian troops from Syria. The move was unexpected and has raised questions as to whether Russia will really pull its forces out of Syria and what might have prompted the decision to announce the withdrawal and, as always, the market implications of the decision were discussed.[46]

---

[43] Adamsky , "Putin's Syria Strategy: Russian Airstrikes and What Comes Next", Foreign Affairs, October 1, 2015, p 1, available online at; https://w ww.foreignaffairs.com/articles/syria/2015-10-01/putins-syria-strategy

[44] Amnesty International, "Russia's Statements on its attacks in Syria unmasked", Amnesty International Report 2015, pp.7-8,

[45] Genevieve Casagrande, "Russian Airstrikes in Syria: November 30 - December 6, 2015", Institute for the Study of War, December 8, 2015, p.1, available online at; http://www.understandingwar.org/backgrounder/russian-airstrikes-syria-november-30-december-6-2015

[46] O'Grady Bill, "The Russian Withdrawal", Advisor Perspectives, March 22, 2016, p.1

However, the question that has risen all over the international area after Russian's sudden withdrawal is "what remained in Syria?". As the departure of Russian forces from Syria already continues, the evidences of constructions at Russia's main air bases in the country demonstrate Moscow's intention to keep an eye on the strong military presence there. Particularly, at the air base in Latakia province and the naval base at Tartus. Having declared victory while maintaining its war-fighting capacity in Syria, Russia has left key questions unanswered: Will it reduce its military role and, if so, to what extent, where and against whom? [47]

The game that Russia is playing in the region by using the ISIS threat has created another dangerous relation. Despite significant cooperation with Turkey in Syria, Russia has continuously provided diplomatic channels for the PYD, which Turkey considers a terrorist organization, therefore Ankara feels uncomfortable with Moscow's non-transparent dialogue with the PKK.[48]

Unlike Turkey, the Russians and Israelis are effectively coordinating their Syria policies, both politically on the different pages. Israel does it mainly because it has no choice in the problem, while Russia does it because it neither needs nor wants to open yet another front, in addition to all the other fronts it already opened in and out of the region. However, it is not unimaginable that future developments could test this relation, with either positive or negative results.[49]

8. EUROPE VS. ISIS OR ISIS VS. EUROPE

Foreign fighters have long been a key element of transnational jihadist movements. In the 1980s, foreigners flocked to South Asia to fight alongside the Afghan mujahedeen. The same thing occurred to a lesser extent in Bosnia and Chechnya in the 1990s and again following the invasion of Iraq in 2003. However, the Syrian civil war and the subsequent

---

[47] International crises Group, "Russia's Choice in Syria", Crisis Group Middle East Briefing N.47, Istanbul/New York/Brussels, 29 March 2016, p.1

[48] Özertem, Hasan Selim, "Turkey and Russia: A Fragile Friendship", Turkish Policy Quarterly, Volume:15 No:4, p.134, available onlie at: http://turkishpolicy.com/files/articlepdf/turkey-and-russia-a-fragile-friendship_en_4553.pdf

[49] Magen Zvi, Russia and the Challenges of a Changing Middle East: A View from Israel, Russia and Israel in the Changing Middle East Conference Proceedings, Memorandum No. 129, July 2013, p.32

rise of the ISIS have broken new ground. Never before have jihadi foreign fighters rallied at the speed and scale as they have in the territory that ISIS now controls.[50]

Today, ISIS is using its foreign fighters and safe haven in Iraq and Syria to execute a terror campaign within Europe and support a larger strategy to punish, destabilize, and polarize the West. ISIS's suicide attacks in the various cities of Europe demonstrate that the jihadist threat to Europe is beating domestic and international law enforcement efforts. ISIS is successfully using its safe haven in Iraq and Syria to train hundreds of foreign fighters for external attacks and these terrorists benefit from wide-ranging support networks across the European continent.

The logistical requirements for facilitating European foreign fighter travel into Iraq and Syria can also export those fighters from ISIS's safe havens back to Europe. Individuals motivated by ISIS are active across Europe, particularly in France, Belgium, Germany, and the United Kingdom. ISIS linked attacks and arrests in Europe are different from ISIS's activity in Turkey, which reflects a spillover from ISIS's campaigns in Iraq and Syria as well as ISIS's campaign to attack the West.[51]An official ISIS media outlet affirmed in a publication released in January 2016 that rather than aiming to destabilize Europe through remarkable attacks, ISIS also seeks to worsen tensions between European states, raise defensive requirements within those states, cause an environment of fear, and inflict additional economic damage on Europe. The attacks to European Union states may strengthen voices calling for some exits from the union since some claim that the attacks proved Schengen free movement and lax border controls are a threat to security.

---

[50] Hardin Lang and Muath Al Wari, "The Flow of Foreign Fighters to the Islamic State Assessing the Challenge and the Response", available online at; https://www.americanprogress.org/issues/security/reports/2016/03/17/133566/the-flow-of-foreign-fighters-to-the-islamic-state/, accessed on; 20 January 2017

[51] Gambhir Harleen , "Isis's Campaign in Europe: March 2016", Institute of the Study of War, March 25, 2016, available online at; http://understandingwar.org/backgrounder/isiss-campaign-europe-march-2016#sthash. K9g5rJDF.dpuf,

Therefore, increasing pressure on European security and unity will open opportunities for ISIS to expand attacks to "crusaders".[52] ISIS particularly aims to destabilize Europe through polarization, which it calls "destroying the gray-zone." ISIS hopes the attacks in its name will provoke state and social backlash against Europe's Muslim communities, encouraging radicalization and jihadist recruitment. Such reactions have surfaced due to the attacks in European metropolitans already, as in the instance of "de-Islamizing the West" concept and the American President's suggestion of patrolling Muslim neighborhoods and banning Muslims from entering the U.S during his election campaign.[53] ISIS will likely exploit these actions in order to claim itself as the defender of Muslims in a broader cultural war, furthermore, it likely does so in order to strengthen xenophobic organizations and rhetoric in Europe, thereby fueling anti-Muslim sentiment and encouraging cultural polarization.[54]

In sum, there is much that can be done to reduce the threat of ISIS terrorist attacks in the West. However, almost inevitably, there will be some terrorist attacks in Europe carried out by returnees from Syria or Iraq. Terrorism cannot be destroyed, it can only be controlled by the common efforts of decisive democratic countries. Nevertheless, Europe already has very effective measures in place to reduce the threat of terrorism from ISIS returnees greatly, and it is also better to stop anti-Islam rhetoric as well. Those measures should be improved in cooperation with all actors and, more importantly, these actors must be adequately resourced against to all kind of terror without any discrimination. Still, the average of success cannot be precision. If it is, European counties are doomed to failure and, worse, doomed to an overreaction which will waste resources and cause dangerous policy mistakes.[55]

---

[52] Sanderson Thomas M, "The Paris Attacks: A Strategic Shift by ISIS?", Statement before the House Foreign Affairs Committee Subcommittee on Terrorism, Nonproliferation, and Trade, December 2, 2015, p.3

[53] Diamond Jeremy, "Donald Trump: Ban all Muslim travel to U.S."CNN report, December 8, 2015, available online at; http://edition.cnn.com/2015/12/07/politics/donald-trump-muslim-ban-immigration/,

[54] Institute for the Study of War, Iraq Situation Report: March 15-21, 2016, available online at: http://www.understandingwar.org/sites/default/files/iraq%20SITREP%202016-03-21.pdf,

[55] Byman Daniel, Jeremy Shapiro, "Be Afraid. Be A Little Afraid: The Threat of Terrorism from Western Foreign Fighters in Syria and Iraq", Foreign Policy at Brookings, Policy Paper Number 34, November 2014, pp.22-23

Map 1: ISIS's Foreign Fighters

9. IRAN VS. ISIS

Syria is a symbol of Iranian power in the region. Iran's alliance with the Assad regime allows it to spread out its influence on the Mediterranean coastline. For this reason, when civil war broke out in Syria, Tehran committed itself to support the government with money, equipment and military assistance in secrecy in the beginning. However, in September 2012, Iran admitted that its elite forces was present in Syria to provide advice, moreover, Iran was shipping weapons and personnel to Syria via Iraq.[56] Actually, to preserve Iraq's and Syria's territorial integrity, as far as the ISIS threat is concerned, Iran opted to arm proxy groups and provide political, military, economic and humanitarian aid to Shi'i and Kurdish

---

[56] Charbonneau Louis, "Exclusive: western report—Iran ships arms, personnel to Syria via Iraq", Reuters, 19 Sept. 2012

stakeholders in these countries, mostly weapons and ammunition to the Kurds in Iraq and to the regime armed forces in Syria.[57]

According to Muhammad-Javad Zarif, Iran's foreign minister: "The menace we're facing, and I say we, because no one is spared, is embodied by the hooded men who are ravaging the cradle of civilization."[58] Although he indicates the possibility of rapprochement between Washington and Tehran against ISIS by this rhetoric, actually he sends messages to all the related states in order to warn them against the general threat coming from ISIS. However, under such expressions of concern is a strategy. Although the permanent destabilization of the Arab heartland would probably be a major victory for the ISIS, Iran, as a key ally of the Iraq's Shiites and the Alawite Bashar al-Assad regime, is using ISIS' ascendance in the Middle East to consolidate its power.[59] Though it has had trouble controlling independently-minded Iraqi Shiite leaders, Tehran achieved a definite success since the U.S. withdrawal from the region in 2011. With the rise of ISIS, and the consequent rise of Iranian hard power, Tehran has become noticeably less concerned about Iraqi perceptions and intra-clerical harmony.[60] Unless ISIS tries to establish terrorist cells inside Iran's Sunni minority communities, Tehran might want to pursue the current balance in the Syria and Iraq with its current profile.

Otherwise, to protect its own territorial integrity, Iran may get involved in the regional clashes intensively and more openly. In other words, a new question comes to our attention: Does Iran uses ISIS for its own interests? Shifting the conflict towards the Mediterranean by using ISIS is a way for Iran. This is the critical point for the Iran and ISIS dilemma.

10. TURKEY VS. ISIS

For 2016, it must be said that Turkey has had very rough times in its domestic politics as well as in the international arena. Domestic terrorism had increased in the Eastern part of Turkey, and the military operations attempted to finish Kurdish Workers Party (PKK). However, it is not only the domestic politics, but also the organizational domestic factors that

---

[57] Iran provided weapons to Iraqi Kurds; Baghdad bomb kills 12', Reuters, 27 Aug. 2014
[58] Takeyh Ray, Reuel Marc Gerecht, "Iran's ISIS Trap How Tehran Uses the Terrorist Group to Get Ahead", Foreign Affairs, November 2015, available online at; https://www.foreignaffairs.com/articles/syria/2015-11-15/irans-isis-trap
[59] Ibid
[60] Esfandiary Dina and Ariane Tabatabai, "Iran's ISIS policy", International Affairs 91: 1, 2015, p.8

caused incredible instability. Turkish people had to experience a military coup in 15th of July due to the actions of military members who belonged to a terrorist organization of Gulen movement (FETO). In addition to these security threats, the biggest threat was coming from Turkish Southeastern borders which are controlled by ISIS militants. Thus, Turkish authorities decided to take an action against human rights violations in Syria with the operations that are backed by Free Syrian Army (FSA or in Turkish ÖSO). By this choice, Turkish parliament aimed to diminish the terrorist attacks attempted by ISIS. Nevertheless, with the recent attacks, it can be analyzed that ISIS' intensifying its organizations and attacks in Turkey caused many civilian deaths. What began as another Arab Spring uprising against an autocratic ruler has expanded into a brutal proxy war that has drawn in the regional and the world powers. Most of the players feared the ISIS more than they do the repressive Assad regime and thought "better to have a regime and a state, than not have a state"; this approach runs counter to Turkey's strategy, which has as its centerpiece the ouster of Assad. Turkey, starting from the beginning, without any policy change, argues that defeating the Islamic State is secondary to the overthrowing of the Damascus government and that once Assad is gone, the Islamic extremists will disappear.

However, ISIS is not the primary concern for Turkey. As it was mentioned before, most of the Kurds involved in the battle in Syria are members of the Syrian Kurdish Democratic Union Party (PYD) and its armed fraction PYD which is a branch of Turkey's long-time foe, the PKK that is known as a terrorist organization.

Although PYD is the only serious military force resisting the Islamic State aside from the Syrian Army, the PKK and ISIS are the same for Turkey and it is wrong to see them differently. They need to be dealt with jointly.[61] Since PKK is officially designated as a "terrorist organization" by the U.S. and the European Union, US initially was reluctant to support a group tied to the PKK. However, Americans have done a 180-degree turn, supplying the PYD with arms, ammunition, and food despite Turkey's strong opposition. Another turn came later from US once more and the U.S. defense chief admitted during testimony before a Senate panel that the PYD and YPG are

---

[61] Tabler Andrew J., Soner Cagaptay, The U.S.-PYD-Turkey Puzzle, the Washington Institute for Near East Policy, October 23, 2015, available online at; http://www.washingtoninstitute.org/policy-analysis/view/the-u.s.-pyd-turkey-puzzle

lined to the PKK terror group. Secretary Ash Carter said "yes" when asked by one of the Senators whether the PYD and its military wing, the YPG, are aligned with the outlawed PKK terror group.[62] Turks' other insistences are the "safe zone" that includes the five northern cities that are Idlib, Latakia, Hasakah, Jarablus, and Kobani, a hefty slice of Syrian territory and also a "no fly zone". Meanwhile, for the United States, establishing a safe zone by force would certainly violate international law unless it had UN sanction, which Russia is unlikely to permit.[63] Also, Kurdish allies of US in Kobani see the "safe zone" as just an attempt by Ankara to meddle in Kurdish affairs. Though it has risks, the "no-fly zone" would not be terribly difficult, but in that case the U.S. would essentially be at war with Syria.[64]

As for equally targeting the Islamic State and Assad, even the Turkish public does not support that. Part of this hesitation is the fear that the war will spill over Turkey, something that has already certainly happened. There have been several car bombings and suicide attacks in the Turkish major cities that killed hundreds of civilians and wounded even more. While blaming Syria, PKK/PYD and ISID for these attacks, Turkey repeated her offers regarding the safe zone as the only solution to stop terrorists.[65] In the last decade, even in the beginning of the Syrian civil war, it was argued that Turkey would own, lead and serve the new Middle East.[66] Instead, now there are three enemies for Turkey in Syria where there was only one enemy once; the Assad regime, the PYD and Daesh. Until one or two years ago, there was an autocratic regime in Syria and people seeking their rights.

Now Turkey no longer knows where the bullet comes from.[67] Turkey has little interest in contributing to a proxy war in Syria and has repeatedly urged the international community to intervene in order to put an end to the violence. Accordingly, Turkey has long pushed for a negotiated end

[62] Turkish Anadolu Agency, "US defense chief admits PYD, YPG, PKK link", 28 April 2016, available online at; http://aa.com.tr/en/world/us-defense-chief-admits-pyd-ypg-pkk-link/563332
[63] Zanotti Jim, "Turkey: Background and U.S. Relations in Brief", Congressional Research Service Report, March 18, 2016, p.9
[64] Cale Salih, "Turkey, the Kurds and the fight against Islamic State, European Council on Foreign Relations, September 2015, p.6
[65] Sengupta Anita," Turkey, Syria, and the Islamic State", Observer Research Foundation Issue Brief issue; 136, March 2016, pp.2-5
[66] Barkey Henri J. "Turkey's Syria Predicament" Survival: Global Politics and Strategy. 25 Nov 2014. p.128
[67] Today's Zaman," Turkey says ISIL convoy hit necessary as threat comes near us, 2 February 2014, available online at; htp://www.todayszaman.com/newsDetail_openPrintPage.action? newsId=338305

to the crisis, which has become a nearly impossible goal considering the rise of ISIS. The rise of ISIS only divides the moderate opposition and delays the end of the Syrian civil war. Furthermore, there is no strategic benefit for Turkey in case ISIS makes gains against Kurdistan Regional Government (KRG) in Iraq and Free Syrian Army (FSA) in Syria, which are both the closest allies of Turkey.[68] ISIS shifted its attack campaign in Turkey in 2016 and may intend to provoke broader conflict within Turkey to change Turkish government's attention away from external politics to internal problems.

11. "WAR ON TERROR" MEANS "WAR ON ISIS"

As far as the fight against terror is concerned, the liberation of Raqqa in the year 2017 marked the transition to the post-ISID period in Syria and Iraq. An intensive aerial bombardment by the US-led coalition helped secure victory in Raqqa for the Syrian Democratic Forces (SDF), which was formed in 2015 by the Kurdish Popular Protection Units (YPG) militia and a number of smaller, Arab factions. Since early June, coalition planes have carried out almost 4,000 air strikes on the city. Estimates of the number of casualties vary. The Syrian Observatory for Human Rights, a UK-based monitoring group, said at least 3,250 people had been killed, among them 1,130 civilians. Other groups say the total was higher. The UN estimates about 270,000 people fled their homes during the SDF offensive.[69]

Moving forward, the main item on the region's agenda will be the creation of functional mechanisms capable of preserving the territorial integrity of both countries since there are still security challenges in the region, citing plans to eliminate terrorism and sectarianism. It is currently argued that aggravating rivalries would be counterproductive and that the only real solution is good governance not only in Syria and Iraq but other conflict-ridden countries as well.[70] Whether Western publics have much appetite for supporting that is open to question. All states need to focus on the fact that some terrorist violence can be contained and defeated in detail, but long-lasting victory is not possible until the causes of terrorism itself are mutually addressed as well as sustaining the coordinated fight against all type of terrorist movements.

[68] Judson Sally, Kadır Ustun, "Turkey's Isis Challenge", The SETA Foundation at Washington, D. C., September 2014, p.3

[69] Available online at; http://www.bbc.com/news/world-middle-east-27838034

[70] Counter-terrorism Pitfalls: What the U.S. Fight against ISIS and al-Qaeda Should Avoid, International Crisis Group, 22 March 2017

Syrian civil war in 2013 and ISIS' territorial conquest in 2014 set off a massive human migration which was more than five million as refugees, and another 6.5 million were internally displaced. This facilitated the efforts of ISIS in using the refugee situation in various ways: ISIS used the wave of refugees to beat the efforts to track their terrorist movements since disagreements between Western states about border controls and intelligence sharing, particularly in European Union, will only continue to aid ISIS.[71] Also through terrorist attacks, the group will continue to manipulate Western publics to further polarize populations against the migrants, which will alienate domestic minority groups, particularly Muslims.

In the future, ISIS will continue to rely on returning experienced terrorists from Syria and Iraq to arrange attacks as well as local volunteers who are willing to either help or engage in their own less sophisticated attacks, and even the lone-wolf types.[72] It is all too easy to call for a new intense military action and new security measures, as part of a natural human reaction to the shocking, horrible, brutal events around the world. However, despite these reactions, ISIS will likely continue to attempt attacks not only in Syria and Iraq, but in western countries as well. It is known and generally accepted that, its supporting worldwide networks may enable ISIS's operatives to launch operations in every part of the world to punish members of the anti-ISIS coalition.

To face the ISIS threat, the world must understand that ISIS as well as various other proponents of radicalism, are part of a new chapter in the book of Terrorism. As a non-state actor, ISIS represents a transformative movement in the politics of the Middle East, one that is qualitatively different from its predecessors.[73]

A well-known story in many war areas is the failing of the society's value system and this generalized break down of values is particularly true for the territory controlled by the Islamic State. For nearly thirty years, people in the region have been involved in various forms of black marketing and

---

71 Syrian Refugee Flows Security Risks and Counterterrorism Challenges, Preliminary findings of a House Homeland Security Committee Review, November 2015, p.2

72 Gardner Frank, "Europe Could Feel the Backlash from Jihadist Conflicts," BBC, 30 November 2013, available online at; http://www.bbc.com/news/worldmiddle-east-25155188

73 Gerges Fawaz A. "ISIS and the Third Wave of Jihadism", Current History, December 2014, p.343

smuggling activities for getting around the dictatorships in the region and today to ensure funding of the Islamic State.[74] Economically, The Islamic State has income from oil sales, taxes on businesses and individuals, the sale of captured equipment, the operation of stolen factories, and a variety of more traditional criminal activity such as kidnapping for ransom, looting, extortion and protection money.[75]

ISIS is more than a terrorist group and it is important to keep in mind that ISIS is not Al Qaeda. ISIS-motivated network in the world is well-trained, well-supported, and well-supplied operatives. Their tactics were improved on hot battlefields such as Syrian and Iraqi battlefields, not at terrorist camps or in the caves of the mountains, as was the case for Al Qaeda. Furthermore, many ISIS members are citizens of European Union countries travelling on European documents not the Middle Eastern passports, which gives ISIS an absolute advantage as it raids unexpected targets. Again, ISIS is not just a terrorist group, therefore counterterrorism won't be enough for an organization consisting of more than 30,000 fighters, which is able to field a real army, hold territory in Iraq and Syria, and confront military forces.[76]

Counterterrorist tactics will not be sufficient unless they are settled into a comprehensive, combined strategy that considers the full range of activities, meaning everything from military operations to humanitarian assistance. Now, using military force in Syria and Iraq is essential for beating ISIS, however, a viable political objective is needed.[77] There are broader risks in relying too much on the military operations as an answer to ISIS. To counter ISIS's terrorist attacks, it is better to stabilize the surrounding area firstly, and then find an immediate applicable international solution for the massive number of Syrian refugees who are still in the region.

---

[74] Brisard Jean-Charles, Damien Martinez, "Islamic State: The Economy-Based Terrorist Funding", Thomson Reuters, October 2014, p.6
[75] Barrett Richard, "The Islamic State", November 2014, p.10
[76] Schmid Alex P, "Foreign (Terrorist) Fighter Estimates: Conceptual and Data Issues", ICCT Policy Brief October 2015, p.14
[77] Christopher M. Blanchard, Carla E. Humud, Mary Beth D. Nikitin, "Armed Conflict in Syria: Overview and U.S. Response", Congressional Research Service Report October 9, 2015, p.27

How much territory IS has lost since January 2015

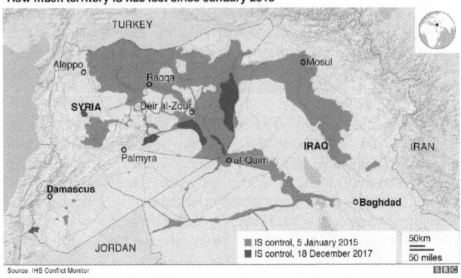

Source: IHS Conflict Monitor

Map 2: IS' territorial loses

Later, in both Syria and Iraq, an extensive strategy needs to be built, developed and implemented that clearly targets ISIS' major assets, specifically its incomes, the flexibility of its forces, its leadership and command structure, its use of social media, and the ongoing regional instability.[78] This will be no short order, of course, but the consequences of not trying are too severe. This is why comprehensive agreements and broad statements of good intentions are sometimes possible, but only because no one takes them seriously. Like many samples in diplomatic arena, they survive the meeting that produces them, however, die upon engagement with reality.[79]

It should also be considered that the failed governance and breakdown of the Syrian state due to the brutal civil war, ISIS threat and external support have enabled the Kurds' Democratic Union Party (PYD) which is an affiliate of the terrorist Kurdistan Worker's Party (PKK), to advance its leftist-nationalist agenda and has been in a political advantage by the open support of United States. However, Kurds do not, on their own, have the

---

[78] Lister Charles, "Profiling the Islamic State", Brookings Doha Center Analysis Paper Number 13, November 2014, p.38

[79] Cordesman Anthony H., "Cooperation in Counterterrorism: Rhetoric vs. Reality", Center for Strategic& International Studies, October 2015, p.1

political or military power to determine the consequence of the conflict or their own future. Both will be up to their relations with other pieces of the Syrian opposition as well as on the arrangements of regional or global powers due to their landlocked position and politics dependent on external patronage.[80]

As far as Turkey's warnings and points regarding the danger of PYD-PKK partnership concerned, new formations may cause new skirmishes in the region. So, what are the implications of these complex dynamics on regional stability, and Syrian end-states? The question remains therefore as to how much damage the Islamic State will be able to inflict before it dies away. Military action will limit its physical reach but will not destroy its appeal either in Iraq and Syria or further afield, unless there is something available to take its place. There is no going back to how things were. The dynamics of the Middle East and its social and political development will all look quite different by the time the ISIS disappears. It is up to the regional powers, helped by the international community, to ensure that what comes afterwards harnesses the energy of dissent in a more positive direction.[81]

Table 2: Changing messy relations in Syria.

	ISIS	TUR	US/EU	SDF	IRAN	RUS	FSA	SYR. Gov.
ISIS	-	E	E	E	E	E	E	E
TURKEY	E	-	F	E	N	N/U	F	E
US/EU	E	F	-	F	E	E	N	E
SDF	E	E	F	-	N/M	F	E	E
IRAN	E	N	E	N/M	-	F	E	F
RUSSIA	E	N/U	N	F	F	-	E	F
FSA	E	F	F	E	E	E	-	E
SYR.Gov.	E	E	E	E	F	F	E	-

(F: Friendly, E: Enemy, N: Neutral, U: Unfriendly, M: Mistrust)

---

[80] Gunes Cengiz, Robert Lowe "The Impact of the Syrian War on Kurdish Politics across the Middle East", Chatham House research paper Middle East and North Africa Programme. July 2015. P.13

[81] Richard Barrett, "The Islamic State", The Soufan Group, November 2014, p.58

The war against ISIS is a critical national security interest for not only the states in the region, but also for the countries worldwide. It not only threatens to create a major center of terrorism and extremism in a critical part of the Middle East, and one that could spread to threaten the flow of energy exports and the global economy, but also to become a major center of international terrorism. It is important to understand, however, that ISIS is not the only cause of instability in the region, and not the only threat caused by spreading sectarian and ethnic violence. Although the political rhetoric about "war" is unavoidable, a formal declaration of war against ISIS with international networks is not very much possible.

As it is noticed the Islamic State has fallen just as quickly as it has ascended, but it very well could maintain its powerful influence in the jihadi world. It means that ISIS may become more dangerous outside and inside Syria and Iraq after those countries are cleared.

• Long-term guerrilla campaigns could continue in Iraq and Syria. Although ISIS has largely been removed from its city strongholds, it remains a presence in sparsely-populated desert areas.

• ISIS leaders and fighters could disperse to its so called other provinces. Libya, Egypt, Afghanistan and Yemen, all have areas held by forces that have declared themselves to be a part of ISIS. Those safe havens for terrorists could be strengthened.

• ISIS fighters could return to their home countries in the Middle East and Europe particularly, and use their experience to mount attacks at home.

• ISIS could become more like Al-Qaeda, inspiring and organizing attacks rather than holding territory and prioritizing the 'far enemy' rather than the 'near enemy' – meaning that European and Asian countries would be more at risk. ISIS has already claimed responsibility for several attacks in Europe.[82] Also the last quarter of the outgoing year witnessed a few spectacular attacks by the Afghan and Pakistan affiliates of the ISID, which raised many eyebrows regarding the group's strength, capability, and future prospects in the region.

---

[82] Smith and Mills, 28

CONCLUSION

The DAESH's strategy was not geared toward negotiating some lasting political solutions, but to exacting ongoing revenge, polarizing societies to exacerbate divisions. The sectarianism in today's Iraq and Syria has been the product of collective action fueled, in part, by "the question of who is a true Muslim and, equally important, who should dominate the Muslim world."[83]

The exaggerated sense of Sunni Arab marginalization, which gave rise to the Islamic State, draws on Sunni political exclusion as well as how the Sunnis collectively perceive the Islamic history and their place in it.[84] Therefore, historicized grievances "whether well-founded or questionable," have provided the easiest way of mobilizing and ultimately weaponing sectarian identities.[85]

Many aspects of the sectarian and ethnic tensions within Iraq and Syria have grown far worse since the beginning of the fighting in each country, and to achieve any lasting form of stability and security is even more difficult. If these issues are not addressed now, there is a serious risk that ISIS may only be the prelude to far worse problems. Both the West and the Muslim states have focused too narrowly on the symptoms of ISIS extremism rather than curing the disease. Movements like ISIS are the symptoms of the disease of terrorism, and not the cause.[86] Thus, the rhetoric of cooperation in counterterrorism comes easily while the reality comes hard since the nations have very different views of who is a terrorist and who is a freedom fighter. While all nations at least claim to oppose terrorism as they individually define it, they do not agree on who should be called a terrorist, on the relative priority for counterterrorism over human rights and civil liberties, or the priorities that should be given to a specific threat.

---

83 Ofra Bengio and Meir Litvak, *Sunna and Shi'a in History: Division and Ecumenism in the Muslim Middle East* (Gordonsville, VA: Palgrave Macmillan, 2011), pp. 1-16. The notion of collective action refers to Craig Calhoun, "The Problem of Identity in Collective Action," in Joan Huber, ed., *Macro-Micro Linkages in Sociology* (Newbury Park, Calif.: Sage, 1991), as cited in Rogers Brubaker, *Nationalism Reframed: Nationhood and the national question in the New Europe* (Cambridge University Press, 1996), fn. 16, p. 20.

84 Brandon Friedman, Uzi Rabi, Sectarianism and War in Iraq and Syria, available online at; http://www.fpri.org/article/2017/01/sectarianism-war-iraq-syria/, accessed on; 22 January 2017

85 Jeremy Black, Clio's Battles: Historiography in Practice (Bloomington, IN: Indiana University Press, 2015), pp. 216-219.

86 Cordesman, 67.

The Influence of the Brexit Process on the Banking System in Romania

Octav NEGURIȚĂ[1]

Abstract

The possible exit of Great Britain from European Union, even in the context of a relatively special status of British banking sector within the Community banking system, cannot remain without effects on the European financial system and thus on the Romanian banking system. The future process of adopting the euro in Romania will bring some changes, as it demands to transform certain mechanisms within the Community's financial and banking system. At European institutional level, the notion that a financial integration at Community level being not complete without the adoption of the single European currency is becoming more and more prevalent. It should not be ignored that the exit of this bloc from the community block may have possible effects on the foreign currency loans market. Similarly on the loans in *lei* too, even when we ignore less developed nature of interbank foreign exchange market. Changing interest rates as a policy instrument of monetary policy, both at the ECB level and at the NBR level will have limited effect.

Keywords: *Negotiation, eurozone, convergence, solvency, vulnerabilities*

[1] *PhD and Assoc. Prof of Financial and Accounting Management, Spiru Haret University, Bucharest.*
E-mail: octavnegurita@yahoo.com

INTRODUCTION

One of the most important consequences concerns the current principle of freedom to provide services directly on the territory of a Member State on the basis of the "EU passport". If, at present, United Kingdom membership of the European Union grants credit institutions and other financial institutions authorized and supervised by the competent UK authority the possibility of providing services on the territory of Romania (or on the territory of other Member States) through the establishment of branches or through the provision of services directly on the basis of a simple notification to the National Bank of Romania by the competent authority of the home Member State, upon leaving the European Union, this privilege will become inapplicable - which would hinder or discourage this type of service between Romania and the United Kingdom.

In other words, in order to provide services on the Romanian territory, in the absence of an "EU passport", credit institutions and other financial institutions in the UK will have to go through a much more difficult process of authorization, complex in terms of documentation and time, but also more expensive in order to achieve the necessary authorization from the National Bank of Romania.

Also, we must not ignore the loss of privileges with regard to the free movement of capital, such as the privilege of cross-border payments within the European Union, according to which the fees charged for cross-border payments within the European Union are the same as those charged for payments made in the same currency within a Member State. This principle will no longer apply between the UK and Romania with the withdrawal of the UK from the European Union. It is also worth recalling the possible impact on the principle of recognition of a judicial decision given in a Member State in the other EU Member States without the need for any special procedure in this regard, particularly considering the enforceability of the guarantee contracts governed by the Romanian law that secures loans governed by English law.

SYSTEMIC RISKS ON THE ROMANIAN BANKING SECTOR

Although they will only be felt after 2019, when Britain's outflow from the European Union will actually be consumed, Brexit's effects on Romania and other Central and Eastern European countries are not very well known considering the future of their economies, depending on the strength of their growth. For Romania, theoretical losses of European structural and cohesion funds are estimated at 300-500 million euros annually as a result of Brexit, but they could only materialize after 2020. Romania has so far attracted some 15 billion euros, especially as a result of intensified efforts in recent years and reached an absorption rate of 82%.

It is expected that the EU budget "after Brexit" will have the same dimension and the EU members will have to increase their contribution, considering the financial agreement between EU and United Kingdom. Thus, Romania has, theoretically, to increase its contribution, affecting the beneficiaries of European funds in the region, the intensity of impact being not very well known. The Romanian government is based on a total financial allocation of about 31 billion euros from the Structural and Investment Funds (SIF), but for the period of 2014-2023, also after the effects of Brexit become reality.

In its financial stability reports, the National Bank of Romania (NBR) says Brexit's systemic risk is moderate. This can mean a lot in the coded terminology of the NBR. Although the implications will only be limited to the near future, Romania will have to calibrate its medium and long-term policies on the basis of the major challenges facing the EU. Brexit remains a factor of uncertainty, especially with regard to the long-term impact, largely depending on the outcome of the negotiations between the EU and the UK. As for the confidence in the euro, recent data show a reduction in Euroscepticism and an increase in consensus on the need to continue reforms to strengthen the institutional and economic framework of the EU.

For Romania, the difficulties in reforming euro area design and policies represent an important impediment to the extent that they are a disruptive factor in the EU's economic redeployment. An economic quasi-stagnation of the Eurozone for a longer period would seriously affect the economic growth capacity in Romania. One reason would be that our economy is low in relation to the euro area. It is therefore absolutely necessary for the Banking Union to have a more alert development on all the basic components, in order EU's euro area policies to be better outlined.

ROMANIA'S DEGREE OF INVOLVEMENT IN THE EUROPEAN SINGLE CURRENCY PROJECT

Starting in July 2015, Romania has met all the nominal convergence criteria linked to the inflation rate, the consolidated budget deficit, the government debt, the exchange rate against the euro and the long-term interest rates. Any departure from these conditions implies the prolongation of the ERM II period accordingly. In this context, ensuring the maintenance of macroeconomic equilibrium in the medium term has positive implications on the convergence process in addition to offering credibility to Romania when it has decided to start the process of joining the European monetary area.

According to the theory of optimal monetary areas, the cost-benefit balance of adopting a single currency depends, to a large extent, on the reduction of the development gaps between the states that form the Monetary Union and the compatibility between them, from the point of view of the economic structure, the degree of commercial integration or the synchronization business cycles in these economies. Therefore, in order to benefit from the adoption of the euro, it is not enough to meet, in a narrow sense, the Maastricht criteria. In fact, there is a need for a durable - and not accidental, forced or temporary - fulfilment of the nominal convergence criteria, which means the necessity to create the conditions for real convergence.

The NBR is fully integrated into the European System of Central Banks, and since 2011, the NBR has set up a Euro Preparation Committee. The adoption of the single currency is not simply a change of banknote, but a complex process involving primarily a political decision based on internal consensus and in agreement with the euro area partners. There is a need for a road map that will result in a target date as an anchor. Such a roadmap involves staging before entry into ERM II during the ERM II period and after entry into the euro area (Voinea, 2015). Assuming that Romania is ready to join today, it would take at least three and a half years to observe all the technical steps.

For Romania, it is vital that the European project does not fall apart; it is also important that Romania, over time, joins the EU's economic and political core, admitting that there will be a variable geometry after Brexit.

This strategic goal at the scale of history involves joining the Eurozone. However, joining the euro area, which is provided in the EU Accession Treaty and in the EU Treaty on the Functioning of the EU (TFEU), must be a rational decision, considering the lessons of the past decades and the major challenges faced by the EU.

EVOLUTION OF THE ROMANIAN BANKING SYSTEM CONSIDERING THE BREXIT STAGES

At aggregate level, between 2016 and 2017, the Romanian banking sector experienced a comfortable level of solvency. However, this general positive image has important nuances. First, the level 1 own funds in Romania is at the level of the EU average. In addition, there is a slight downward trend (from 16.4 percent in December 2015 to 16.1 percent in September 2016 and to 16.0 in October 2017). Under these circumstances, any measures to preserve and increase the solvency of the Romanian banking sector could not be interpreted as excessive compared to the European situation.

The Romanian banking system has prudential indicators of solvency, profitability and balance sheet structure better than the European average, while the quality of shareholders is discordant due to the low and bad credit rates with restructuring measures that are more than double the EU average. The prudential indicators of the Romanian banking system (solvency, coverage rate, profitability, balance sheet structure) are generally better than the European average, with two exceptions - the rate of bad loans and the restructuring rate. The European Banking Authority (EBA) publishes on a quarterly analysis (Risk Dashboard) which presents the main vulnerabilities of the European banking sector identified by the evolution of a set of risk indicators. The indicators are grouped into four categories: solvency, asset quality, profitability and balance sheet structure. And each indicator is evaluated against three prudence intervals, so its value can be considered very good, intermediate or deficient depending on the value range it belongs to.

The rate of bad debts and of loans with restructuring measures remain in the value band considered by the European Banking Authority to be "deficient", the level of these indicators being more than double the EU average. The non-performing loans (NPL) at the level of the entire banking system reached around 13% at the end of March, continuing the downward trend last year. Bank balances have started to look better starting with the second half of 2014, improving the quality of portfolios as a result of troubled loan sales. However, the two vulnerabilities are diminished by the third indicator of asset quality analysis, namely the coverage ratio with non-performing loans, which places the Romanian banking system at the most prudent value range, over 58%, well above the average European, about 44%.

The financial health of the banking sector continue to remain robust. Solvency ratios remain at appropriate levels around the European average. Consistent capital buffers vs. prudential requirements provide good absorption capacity for unexpected losses and resources for lending to the real sector.

The balance sheet structure remained balanced in the first quarter of this year, respecting both the ratio of loans and deposits (around 80%) to total debt and equity (around 8%). The solvency ratios, which show how well the bank system is capitalized, maintain a high level for the best prudence range, slightly increasing over the past three years.

The results of stress testing of the banking sector reveal robustness at aggregate level in the event of adverse macroeconomic scenarios. The impact of the interest rate risk on the banking sector is important due to the longer-term asset structure, considering the backdrop of an important weight of fixed income items. The profitability of the banking sector has improved in the context of a favorable domestic macroeconomic framework, a significant reduction in net expenditures with depreciation adjustments, a prolongation of low financing costs, and a recovery in domestic currency lending. So we can say that the adoption process has not been influenced in this context, at least at the level of the process of adopting banking policies at national level.

The consolidation process of the Romanian banking sector continued in 2017, but at a slower pace. The outlook is accentuated, considering the strategic decisions of some banking groups present in Romania in order to limit exposure in certain markets and the need to improve operational efficiency. The structural vulnerabilities of the reported banks' balance sheet, such as: (i) non-maturity mismatch of sources attracted to financial assets, or (ii) existing currency imbalances in which bank assets and liabilities are denominated, continued to be remedied.

For the banking sector as a whole, the balance sheet structure does not raise concerns considering the ratio between total debt and equity, which is within a prudent range, according to criteria established by the European Banking Authority. However, the ratio between loans and deposits continued to decline, and if these dynamics persist, risks may arise from a macro-prudential perspective (generated by the significant under-utilization of the resources that banks attract from the economy).

During the economic and financial crisis, Romania did not have to support the banking sector with public money, and the shareholders of the banks contributed to the additional capital. In 2008-2016, an equity of 3.5 billion euros was raised by banks. The years 2016-2017 were, for the banking market, the first years of return to a real operational profitability that it didn't have for a few years, amid the reduction in the cost of risk. ROA has registered over 1.00% and ROE has reached over 10.00%.

The banking sector performed well over the past year, as the process of optimizing the quality of the asset portfolio continued. The present rate of non-performing loans was down by 2.3 times to the maximum that was recorded in 2014. These are the indicators that show the long-term effectiveness of how money is used, namely own money or borrowed money through deposits or loans. In addition, the level at which the banking system in Romania is located is very high. It can show healthy activity, but at the same time the selling of expensive credits. The banking system has grown since lending activity has accelerated, especially for individuals.

The rate of non-performing loans as defined by the EBA has decreased to 9.46% at the end of December, 2016 and later to 8.32% in June, 2017. Thus, we continue to see a reduction in the non-performing loans ratio to the middle zone of the range, both through the stock-market balancing operations of the banking system and by reviving the secondary market for the sale of collateral in various execution phases. Capital requirements have increased, new liquidity rules have been introduced with an impact on the maturity of the asset structure, and credit risk assessment is much closer.

Considering this background, there is an orderly withdrawal mainly due to the absence of investment opportunities or less favorable return on capital. Thus, we can say that Romania has overcome the danger of disorderly withdrawals that have affected bank financing in the years of crisis, but the tendency to reduce exposure is still present. Under these circumstances, it is the responsibility of banks to secure their financing from local sources, and the fact that the banking system in Romania has returned to profit, even more operational profitability, is a very good indicator of these risks.

The increased limited availability of external financing for the Romanian banking markets indicates that deposits will have a relative attractiveness in the following years. As a result, the sustained increase in the volume of credit in Romania will be more closely linked to the increase in the volume of deposits. Moreover, some Eastern and Central European economies may experience a prolonged slow growth in the volume of credits. Credit-to-GDP ratios have relatively high levels in some CEE economies where incomes are lower. Moreover, certain market segments, such as consumer lending segment, do not appear to be underdeveloped in the Romanian economy. Consequently, credit growth in Romania will not be the same as in the last decade. Even though Central and Eastern European (CEE) lending growth rates will not be the same as in the last ten years, medium and long-term prospects for the banking sector remain extremely favorable.

POSSIBLE REASONS FOR THE SLOWING IN THE ADOPTION OF EURO BY ROMANIA IN THE CONTEXT OF BREXIT PROCESS

One of the factors that could lead to a delay in the adoption of the euro could be even negative repercussions on national economic developments. Romania recorded one of the highest economic growth rates in the EU in 2017, the main determinant being domestic consumption, while the trade balance, the public deficit and the inflation rate deteriorated. Investments did not make a significant contribution to the economic growth. These developments indicate the build-up of tensions with potentially significant negative consequences on future economic activity and implicitly on the financial stability.

An important factor in resuming the economic growth was the revitalization of global trade. Nevertheless, the risks of strengthening the growth rate of the global economy and of the international trade remain important, due to policies uncertainty, the accumulation of structural imbalances in emerging economies and the intensification of geopolitical tensions. International financial markets recorded positive developments in the first half of 2017 after the corrections recorded at the end of 2016, while volatility was on a downward trend with short growth periods.

An important systemic risk to financial stability in Romania, similar to the systemic risk at EU level, is related to the abrupt adjustment of the risk premium for emerging countries. In order to increase the role of the financial system over long-term economic growth, it is necessary to address these structural problems. As regards public sector indebtedness, the credibility of the implemented economic policies and the responsibility in managing public finances are important elements in ensuring investor confidence and implicitly a low cost of public debt financing. Recent developments do not indicate problems with the sustainability of external debt in the short term.

The refinancing risk decreased as the average maturity increased. Foreign FDI flows provided much of the funding needed for the current account deficit. An important systemic risk to financial stability in Romania, similar to that at EU level, is the general adjustment of the risk premium for emerging economies. The implementation of a policy mix that is conducive to maintaining macroeconomic balances represents an important condition for limiting the contagion effects from international financial markets, given the risk of a sudden change in investor confidence in emerging economies.

Brexit remains a factor of uncertainty, especially with regard to the long-term impact, largely depending on the outcome of the negotiations between the EU and the UK. As for the Romanians confidence in the euro, recent data show a reduction in Euroscepticism and an increase in consensus on the need to continue reforms to strengthen the institutional and economic framework of the EU. Europe's bank profitability slightly improved in the first half of 2017. Thus, return on equity (ROE) rose by 3.7 percentage points in the second quarter of 2017 compared to the last quarter of 2016, reaching 7 percent. Also, return on assets (ROA) rose to 0.45 percent over the same period, from 0.21 percent at the end of 2016.

Romania is among the countries with the highest level of banking profitability, along with other countries in the region. Romania recorded one of the highest economic growth rates in the EU in 2017. However, the analysis of the main macroeconomic indicators reveals the accumulation of tensions, with potentially significant negative consequences on future economic developments and implicitly on financial stability. Against this background, the continuation of the convergence process is conditioned by the recalibration of the policy mix so as to ensure the sustainability of the fundamental economic indicators.

Cooperation between institutions having a role in the coordination of economic policies is essential for achieving an optimal mix of policies for the Romanian economy. Until now, Romania has gone through a continuous process of convergence, even during the economic crisis. However, inflationary tensions and budget deficits have accumulated.

A critical mass of companies has been formed in Romania to meet the challenges of eventual joining the Eurozone. According to the recent developments (Neagu et al., 2017), the number of companies making the critical mass is relatively low (below 10 percent of the total number of active companies in the economy). These companies have recorded higher economic and financial performance indicators than the rest of the economy and are the basis for a sustainable economic growth. Thus, we can say that the activity of the Romanian economic societies was not negatively influenced, even in the current context of the post-Brexit negotiations, in the conditions in which the trade balance with the UK was one of the few with which Romania has a favorable value to our country.

It should not be overlooked that the Eurozone itself has to go through the reform process. In order to complete the Banking Union, the European Deposit Guarantee Scheme (EDIS) must be operational, minimum own funds and eligible debt requirements (MRELs) must be established. Also, it has to clarify the contradiction between bank micro-prudential consolidated supervision and the national responsibility for resolution. There is no consensus either on the creation of the Fiscal Union or on debt mutualisation, while the Union of Capital Markets represents still an early process. Other structural reforms at European level should seek to find a replacement for EURIBOR, should seek to implement unitary rules of transparency, reporting and accountability for buyers of bad credit packages, and should seek to modify the treatment of sovereign exposures in order to recognize the absence of zero risk.

Even if there are, at least partly justified, opinions on adopting other types of criteria regarding Romania's capacity to adopt the euro, we cannot ignore the basic principles regarding the adoption of the euro by any state. Along with six other countries (Bulgaria, the Czech Republic, Croatia, Poland, Sweden, Hungary), Romania is among the Member States of the European Union which have the obligation to adopt the euro, which means, in practice, full participation in the Economic and Monetary Union, once all the necessary conditions have been met, namely the nominal, legal and real convergence criteria. The latter are not explicitly mentioned in the relevant EU legislation, but they are becoming more and more important in assessing the state's readiness for the adoption of the single currency.

In fact, the Convergence Reports, developed every two years by the European Central Bank and the European Commission, are increasingly focusing on real convergence. Thus, in the run-up to the adoption of the single currency, the national economy must undergo the necessary adjustments to the euro area, marked by broad structural reforms, with effects on its overall competitiveness.

At the time of the drafting of the 2016 Convergence Report of the European Central Bank, Romania fulfilled all the criteria of nominal convergence and only part of the criteria of legal convergence. The 2017-2020 Convergence Program states that the Romanian Government remains committed to joining the Eurozone, but the establishment of a concrete date in this regard requires the carrying out of in-depth analyses, especially regarding the real, structural and institutional convergence areas where major progress is needed.

From the data set out in the ECB 2016 Convergence Report, we can conclude that the Romanian economy was not influenced by the UK dictatorship of leaving the EU, the trend of macroeconomic indications being relevant in this respect. Also, the observations made regarding the evolution of these indicators refer only to the influences of domestic economic problems in Romania and not to external influences, whether they are ecological, political or social.

The average annual HICP inflation recorded by Romania in the last 10 years fluctuated within a relatively wide range, ranging from -1.3% to 8.5% and the average of the period were at a high level of 4.5%. Looking ahead, there are concerns about the sustainability of inflation convergence in Romania for a longer period. It is likely that the gap recovery process will lead to positive inflation differentials in relation to Eurozone.

In Romania, the budget deficit and public debt fell to the levels set by the Maastricht criteria. Romania is the object of the preventive component of the Stability and Growth Pact from 2013 onwards. According to the Ministry of Finance reports, the budget deficit in 2017 registered a share of 2.83% of GDP, below the 3% of GDP ceiling for the budget deficit.

During the 10 years spent as a member of the U.E., the Romanian currency did not participate in ERM II, but was traded under a flexible floating rate regime. The exchange rate of the Romanian currency in relation to euro currency has, on average, displayed a relatively high degree of volatility in the reference period. The cumulative balance of Romania's current and capital account has experienced substantial improvement over the past 10 years, but the value of net external liabilities, although gradually narrowing, remains at high levels. Also, in the reference period May 2015 - April 2017, long-term interest rates were on average 3.6% lower than the benchmark of 4.0% on the benchmark interest rate convergence criterion.

In Romania, long-term interest rates have been on a declining trend since 2009, with 12-month average rates falling from around 10% to below 4%. On a legislative level, Romania still does not fulfil all the central bank independence requirements, the ban on monetary financing and the legal integration of the central bank in the Euro-system. However, our country is subject to derogation and must therefore comply with all the adaptation requirements laid down in Article 131 of the Treaty.

Thus, it is questionable which of the indicators could be most affected by the UK detachment from the EU. Probably the only indicators influenced in this sense would be the budget deficit and the public debt. At budget level, at least until the 2020 horizon, Romania would not have any influence because the United Kingdom will participate with the same amount in the European Union budget, and after that year it will be registering budget regressive budgets. By 2020, the only problem that can arise will be to increase the capacity of our country to absorb the available Community funds, a problematic point in this context. If our country succeeds, even to a lesser extent, in increasing the absorption of EU funds, Romania's budget will not be influenced by the increase of our country's contributions to the EU budget that will take place after 2020.

Another aspect is the evolution of the trade relationship that our country has with the UK, a relationship that has led to a positive balance for our country as well as one of the only ones registered with the U.E. It is obvious that the UK will want to sustain, at least at the same pace, the trade relations with the EU Member States, a reason for this being the negotiations for a trade agreement valid after the UK's effective exit from the EU. The vote in 2016 did not trigger an inversion of Romania-UK trade relations, with the figures even recording an increase in import-export volumes.

Romania has reached a certain degree of real convergence with the EU. There are, of course, great gaps in the degree of economic development (GDP / inhabitant), in the structure of the economy, in the quality of the infrastructure, the functioning of the institutions, the living standards, etc., but Romania's foreign trade is mainly carried out with the other EU countries. This reorientation of foreign trade over the past two decades has been largely determined by foreign direct investment, which, although smaller than other countries in the region, is the main source of foreign financing for the Romanian economy. As a result of this factor's action, in terms of commercial integration (the common market), Romania is more integrated into the EU than it was when countries like Greece, Portugal and Spain joined the EMU.

Romania participates in the "European System of Payments in Euros" - TARGET 2 and started to implement some elements of the "European Banking Union" - UEB (the single regulatory framework on capital requirements, the "Unique Resolution Mechanism" URM, European Deposit Guarantee Fund "- EDGF, etc.). In other words, we could say that Romania is already in a rather advanced phase of financial integration in the euro area. In this context, highlighting the difficulties and the risks of the early adoption of the euro seems overly negative. There is fear that by adopting the euro the real interest rates in Romania would become smaller than the equilibrium ones, which would lead to the artificial growth of credit and the emergence of speculative bubbles in real estate. However, the interest rate (real or nominal) is a theoretical size, not an observable size.

The assertion that actual interest rates on the market are or will be lower, equal to or higher than the equilibrium level, cannot be verified empirically even before and especially in the next period. Second, equilibrium interest is not a forever given size because demand and supply of credit are constantly changing. In Romania, the credit supply comes mainly from subsidiaries and branches of foreign banks whose head office is located in Eurozone countries and are already subject to the UEB and single monetary policy. Finally, lowering interest rates stimulates investment and, therefore, economic growth, which is exactly what Romania needs to do to recover the gaps.

There is also the idea that accession to the euro-zone could be hindered by the appreciation of the evolution of Brexit, which would have negative effects on the external competitiveness of the Romanian economy. Such an evolution is unlikely to be due to the current account deficit and the decrease in capital inflows. The evolution of the past two years denies this theory, the Romanian currency showing a downward trend towards the euro starting with the third quarter of 2016 against the British currency. Since the financial crisis, the Romanian currency has remained in the stability claimed by the exchange rate mechanism II (ERM II), indeed with a support from the IMF loan, instead of the ECB's support, this being the best credibility element that the Romanian economy can cope with the requirements of the euro adoption.

Romania's decision to move to the euro has to come together with others, which set a much wider framework of Union issues and policies if it is to draw a realistic perspective of the process of European integration. The Union has reached a high degree of complexity. The package decision to adopt the single currency must be based ab-initio and on the option of a fundamental approach to the opportunities of the moment. Perhaps their optimal use is related to the way we see the resolution of the crisis of the Union nucleus, the European Monetary Union.

The problem is not whether Romania needs to adopt the euro or not, but whether it gains more benefits by waiting or entering EMU quickly. In principle, in relation to this issue, as with other aspects of the post-communist era, two positions can be formulated: "gradualism" or "shock therapy". According to the first position, entry into the EMU should be the result of a long process of real convergence of the Romanian economy. The arguments of the advocates of this position are based on highlighting the many stringent conditions on which it depends - beyond the Maastricht criteria of convergence - the successful adoption of the euro. According to the second position, to which we subscribe, the adoption of the euro must be done as quickly as possible, since membership in the EMU favors a faster real convergence of the economy and thus, an easier recovery of the immense gaps that separate Romania from the developed part of Europe. As a result, the main issue is not the fulfillment of economic or technical criteria, but the politics abandoning the autonomy of national monetary policy and competently and responsibly participating in the work of developing and implementing the common monetary policy.

CONCLUSION

As far as Romania is concerned, the prospect of preserving the net income (in a generic sense), which is otherwise necessary, requires a serious internal structural fiscal reform (budget revenue is only 28% of GDP), to provide complementary resources, not only following the outbreak of the UK, but also of the restructuring of the Union's funded objectives and, possibly, the increase in co-financing, which makes the access to Union funds conditional. The most relevant example, namely the idea we must become more accustomed to if we want more public goods and services from the Union is investing in our capacity and solidity to offer them.

Reforming the European Union, especially in the context of Brexit's production, is a great opportunity for Romania to get out of a shadow of passivity that is otherwise recognized. The balance of the 10th anniversary of joining with the good and the less good, and the way we should see the participation in the European integration process until now offer us serious arguments to put strong themes of mutual interest in the negotiation bases much more balanced.

As a political project, the euro was a complex investment with multiple and large initial costs up to its physical realization (currency in circulation, issuing bank, price stability mandate), putting it into circulation and supporting its course towards the vicissitudes of the complex environment (renouncing national monetary policy, renouncing national currencies, a single monetary policy and even survival with the disadvantages of a single monetary policy in the absence of a fiscal pillar, etc.). The euro could not be thought of without benefits, and these - along with the costs - cannot be reduced to a simple mathematics. Recovering the initial "investment" for the single currency is itself the completion of the European project, a process in which Romania is hired as a Member State, and the option of completing its own European project, as a Member State, cannot be cost-benefit-related mathematically determined, but only by what the Union wants with Romania at the table of its decisions.

The legal exemption granted by Romania, with no expiry date, cannot be interpreted as permanent (unlike the express and explicit cases of Great Britain and Denmark, but may be modified) and therefore the "obligation" of the euro adoption cannot be challenged for economic reasons or political considerations ex post signing the Accession Treaty interpreted as disadvantages or eventually high opportunity costs, when in fact the choice of the moment is the right of the Member State without being exercised on a certain date.

REFERENCES

[1] Cerna, S. (2016). De ce să amânăm trecerea la adoptarea euro? Trecerea la euro în 2019 este posibilă și ar putea fin un moment astral în istoria recentă a României. Retrieved from http://www.zf.ro/opinii/de-ce-sa-amanam-adoptarea-euro-trecerea-la-euro-in-2019-este-posibila-si-ar-putea-fi-un-moment-astral-in-istoria-recenta-a-romaniei-15740711 accessed on 20.08.2017.

[2] Dăianu, D., Kallai, E., & Socol, A. (2017). România și aderarea la zona euro: întrebarea este, ÎN CE CONDIȚII. Retrieved from http://zbw.eu/econis-archiv/bitstream/handle/11159/153/Studiu_euro_SPOS_2016.pdf?sequence=1&isAllowed=y accesed on 29.01.2017

[3] European Central Bank. (2016). Raport de convergență Iunie 2016. Retrieved from http://www.ecb.europa.eu/pub/pdf/conrep/cr201606.ro.pdf?2c4cc232f10de64f1976b9ffda2abc74 accesed on 21.01.2017

[4] Ionescu, A. (2017). România și BREXIT: Pagubele Bucureștiului în comparație cu țările Europei Centrale și de Est. Efecte limitate pe termen scurt, mari amenințări pe termen lung. Retrieved from http://cursdeguvernare.ro/romania-si-brexit-pagubele-bucurestiului-in-comparatie-cu-tarile-europei-centrale-si-de-est-efecte-limitate-pe-termen-scurt-mari-amenintari-pe-termen-lung.html accesed on 21.11.2017.

[5] Medrega, C. (2016). Sistemul bancar românesc este cu mult peste media UE la mai mulți indicatori de risc, cu excepția ratei creditelor neperformante și cea a creditelor restructurate. Retrieved from http://www.zf.ro/banci-si-asigurari/sistemul-bancar-romanesc-este-cu-mult-peste-media-ue-la-mai-multi-indicatori-de-risc-cu-exceptia-ratei-creditelor-neperformante-si-cea-a-creditelor-restructurate-15500706 accessed on 25.09.2017.

[6] Moloney, N. (2017). Financial services, the EU, and Brexit: an uncertain future for the city?. LSE Reasearch Online. Retrieved from http://eprints. lse.ac.uk/67292/1/Moloney_Financial_Services_the_EU_and_Brexit.pdf accesed on 08.12.2017.

[7] Muşat & Asociaţii Analyse. (2016). Impactul pentru bănci, burse, concurenţă, drept comercial, dreptul muncii şi fiscalitat. Retrieved from http://www.zf.ro/banci-si-asigurari/analiza-brexit-musat-asociatii-impactul-pentru-banci-burse-concurenta-drept-comercial-dreptul-muncii-si-fiscalitate-15519922 accesed on 12.12.2017.

[8] National Bank of Romania. (2017). Raport asupra stabilităţii financare decembrie 2017. Retrieved from http://www.bnr.ro/DocumentInformation. aspx?idDocument=26693&idInfoClass=19966 accesed on 07.01.2018.

[9] National Bank of Romania. (2017). Raport asupra stabilităţii financiare mai 2017. Retrieved from http://www.bnr.ro/DocumentInformation. aspx?idDocument=25183&idInfoClass=19966 accesed on 25.09.2017.

[10] National Bank of Romania. (2017). România şi adoptarea euro. Retrieved from http://www.opiniibnr.ro/content/romania-si-adoptarea-euro.pdf accesed on 30.10.2017.

[11] Neagu, F., Dragu, F., & Costeiu, A. (2017). Pregătiţi pentru viitor? O nouă perspectivă asupra economiei Romaniei. Retrieved from www.bnr.ro%2Ffiles%2Fd%2FPubs_ro%2FCaiete%2F2017cs46. pdf&usg=AOvVaw3xYgx92UrbolewX_QU7quC.

[12] Romanian Banks Association. (2016). Sistemul bancar din România. Retrieved from http://www.arb.ro/sistemul-bancar-din-romania/sistemul-bancar-din-romania/ accesed on 28.11.2017.

[13] Voinea, L. (2015). O perspectivă asupra foii de parcurs pentru adoptarea euro. Preparation committee on the changeover to the euro. National +Bank of Romania.

The Make in India Initiative: Has it Worked?

Lalita SOM[1]

Abstract

Manufacturing sector has the potential to lift half a billion more of India's population out of poverty through income, export and employment growth. For a broad economic growth, India must focus both on domestic production to satisfy its large domestic demand and producing goods for global markets. However, value added manufacturing, as a percentage of GDP, has remained constant since 2000. *Make in India* was launched in 2014 to bring manufacturing back into the spotlight. The article looks at the relevant progress made since the launch of *Make in India*. Since then, the country has improved its rank consistently and has seen a significant jump of 30 places in 2017 in the World Bank's annual ease of doing business survey and has eased statutory restrictions on foreign direct investment across sectors. Consequently, FDI inflows saw a rise, but the investment to GDP and the ratio of value added manufacturing to GDP have been declining. The downward trend in many of the economic variables like the current account has been unambiguous since the beginning of 2017. There is a broad consensus amongst commentators about the downward trend in the economic variables related to manufacturing and the structural impediments facing manufacturing in India. To achieve the objectives of *Make in India*, India must position itself to benefit from the structural changes in technology and other emerging forces of globalization. For this, India needs to address a number of structural bottlenecks, which have intensified India's loss of competitiveness in the manufacturing sector. The article discusses the ten most important of these structural impediments and evaluates the progress India has made since the launch of Make in India and bolsters its arguments with international indices capturing trends in those structural variables. However, it is too early to call *Make in India* a success or a failure. Although India has introduced some significant policy changes, the success of these policies is dependent on their effective implementation.

Keywords: *Make in India, manufacturing value added, factor markets, infrastructure, regulatory bottlenecks.*

[1] Lalita Som has worked for the Organization of Economic Cooperation and Development in Paris. She can be reached at lalita.som@gmail.com.

INTRODUCTION

During 2003-08, a big reason for optimism in the Indian economy was higher capital expenditure by private firms, which rose during that period by 36 percent of GDP. The 26 percent decline in corporate investment since then has been the single biggest cause of India's slowdown.

Value-added manufacturing accounted for only 16.5 percent of India's GDP, compared to the services sector which contributes nearly 53.8 percent to the GDP in 2016 (World Bank, 2017). Manufacturing value-added as a percentage of GDP has remained more or less stagnant since 2000.

In terms of employment, manufacturing has not been a major long-term driver of job creation in India. After fluctuating around 11 percent for some time, it increased quite strongly to 12.6 percent in 2011-12 before declining to 10.7 percent in 2013-14 (ILO,2016). Between 2004-05 and 2011-12, when total employment outside of agriculture rose around 51 million, only 6 million jobs were created in manufacturing. Most of them were informal jobs.

Although, the share of merchandise exports in GDP increased from about 8 percent in 1999–2000 to 16.8 percent in 2013–14, India's share in global merchandise exports has remained low. India represents slightly more than 2 percent of the world's manufacturing output, a tenth of what China contributes.

To capitalize on the demographic dividend, India must create nearly one million jobs per month over the next decade. Manufacturing is seen to have the potential to provide large-scale employment to the young Indian population, at a time when manufacturing jobs are shrinking globally and a new global economic paradigm is emerging, driven by the rapid growth in digital technologies. A McKinsey study finds that rising demand in India, together with the multinationals' desire to diversify their production to include low-cost plants in countries other than China, could together help India's manufacturing sector to grow six-fold by 2025, to $1 trillion and could create up to 90 million domestic jobs (Dhawan, Swaroop & Zainulbhai, 2012).

With this conviction, the current government launched the *Make in India* initiative in 2014, aimed at making India a global manufacturing hub by urging investors to think of India not only as a big emerging market, but also as a place for production. 'Make in India' is designed to facilitate investment, foster innovation, protect intellectual property, and build best-in-class manufacturing infrastructure in India.

The ambitious initiative represented an attitudinal shift in how India relates to investors: not as a permit-issuing authority, but as a facilitator of business and as a business partner. The initiative identified 25 growth sectors, and includes the creation of a website through which companies can seek policy clarifications within 72 hours.

The plan specifically included proposals to cut red tape, develop infrastructure and make it easier for companies to do business. In 2014, India ranked 134th (out of 189 countries) in the World Bank's ease of doing business survey. Measures to reduce complexity and to improve transparency in regulation have been therefore a significant part of the *Make in India* initiative. An investor facilitation team was set up to be the first reference point for guiding foreign investors on all aspects of regulatory and policy issues.

This article looks at the progress that India has made in the last three years since the launch of the *Make in India* initiative and whether economic reforms have strengthened the country's manufacturing ecosystem sufficiently to make it a viable global manufacturing hub.

THE ROLE OF MANUFACTURING IN ECONOMIC GROWTH AND EMPLOYMENT

Since the industrial revolution, almost all countries that have managed the transition from low to high income have undergone industrialization, diversifying and upgrading their production structure, reducing their dependence on agriculture and natural resources. Understanding the channels through which manufacturing growth affects economic growth and employment, is essential to consider how Make in India will mobilize higher labor absorption and lead to better economic outcomes.

Kaldor examined the relationship between industrial development and economic growth, and based on empirical results, characterized the manufacturing sector as "the main engine of fast growth" (Kaldor, 1967). He argued that manufacturing had the capacity to generate 'dynamic increasing returns' i.e. manufacturing not only has the potential to increase its output more than proportionate to the increase in inputs (i.e. increasing returns to scale), but also, the faster the rate of growth of output in manufacturing, the faster the rate of growth of both manufacturing and economy-wide productivity (dynamic increasing returns) (Thirlwall, 1983). This implies that manufacturing is the core driver of GDP growth and employment while the service sector is likely to grow on the basis of the growing demand derived from (and resulting from) an increasing GDP.

This not only was true for the 12 early industrializers Kaldor examined, from UK to Japan, but was also the characteristic of South-east Asian countries that have experienced rapid, sustained growth. The 2008 Commission on Growth and Development identified common features of catching up countries that have achieved 'episodes of high and sustained growth' in excess of 7% per annum for 25 years or more (World Bank,2008). Nine of the thirteen success stories were cases of manufacturing-led growth: Brazil, China, Indonesia, the Republic of Korea, Malaysia, Singapore, Taiwan, China and Thailand. Only a few countries endowed with natural resources, and with small populations, have gone through a period of sustained economic growth without advancing manufacturing production, like Botswana and Oman. In recent years, however, very few countries have achieved such a sustained period of high growth and job creation, other than China.

A number of researchers have tested Kaldor's hypotheses across a range of developing countries (Dasgupta & Singh, 2005) (Wells & Thirlwall, 2003). They found that manufacturing has a positive correlation with GDP growth. Szirmai and Verspagen (2015) tested the relationship between the value-added share of manufacturing and growth of GDP per capita. This relationship was examined for three periods, 1950–1970, 1970–1990 and 1990–2005, and compared with the service sector. It was found that manufacturing acts, as an engine of growth for low and for some middle-income countries, provided they have a sufficient level of human capital. The findings for more recent periods indicate that a higher level of human capital (at least 7-8 years of education) is necessary for manufacturing to play the role of engine of growth in developing countries (Adam & Verspagen, 2015).

In India, Chakravarty and Mitra (2009) found manufacturing to have been one of the drivers of growth, together with construction and services between 1973-2004 period (Chakravarty & Mitra 2009). For the period between 1994-2006, Kathuria and Raj (2013) found that in 15 states manufacturing had indeed acted as an engine of growth in India, despite its declining share in GDP (Vinish & Natarajan, 2013).

India is part of the general trend of premature deindustrialization which is prevalent in developing countries with the share of manufacturing value-added (MVA) relative to that of other sectors and employment decreasing significantly. However, it has been widely witnessed that manufacturing jobs are shrinking globally as the service sector's share of production and employment is large and growing in most advanced and many developing countries. The growth of productivity and of income has historically appeared to slow once factors of production began to shift from manufacturing to services (Baumol,1967). This phenomenon facing the global economy is the 'post-industrial' state in which development does not rely on industrialization. This phenomenon could be especially worrisome for developing economies where employment shares are shifting from agriculture to services, bypassing manufacturing, given that skipping the industrialization phase could constrain their ability to narrow income gaps (Rodrik, 2016).

The model of globalization that shaped the economic growth of countries - from low to medium / high income and that followed the transition from agriculture to light manufacturing and rapid growth of exports, followed by development of heavy industry and then services - has been disrupted today by the growth in digital technologies, including manufacturing technologies. These new technologies are resulting in large-scale manufacturing and global merchandise exports losing their primacy as drivers of growth and jobs in the medium to longer term. In addition, the competitiveness of countries with low cost labor advantage is eroding due to growing local regulation and protectionism. Given these global policy and technology shifts, is India's focus both on domestically-oriented production to satisfy large domestic demand and producing goods for global markets a viable economic model? Although a stronger manufacturing sector could help link India to global supply chains, boost exports, and create jobs, is Make in India too little, too late? India needs to adapt its policies to reflect the changing nature of the industry and accommodate changes over many policy areas simultaneously.

MAKE IN INDIA AND ITS PROGRESS SINCE THE LAUNCH
Despite the advantage of low level wages and the rapidly eroding availability of abundant labor force, there is unanimity in that India would have to compete against most countries in the production and export of manufactured goods. Whereas India has been unable to do so; so far it is due to rigid labor and taxation laws, difficult process of land acquisition, regulation, and poor infrastructure; all of these have been significant constraints in achieving higher growth targets.

Nonetheless, over the past decade, the country's auto industry has been an exception to the general decline in manufacturing. According to the Society of Indian Automobile Manufacturers (SIAM), in terms of output—more than 3 million cars have been produced in India since 2011-12. In the mid-1990s, India opened its automobile industry for the investments of foreign manufacturers. By the early 2000s, India had become a global source for auto-components supplying global car manufacturers for their local as well as global supply chains. In the late 2000s, Indian automakers began to acquire auto companies overseas. Participation of foreign manufacturers provided the technology in making Indian parts and vehicles competent with global standards. In 2004, India produced 1.18 million cars, and by the end of 2016, it produced 3.68 million cars. The auto industry contributes 7 percent of GDP and employs, directly or indirectly, around 19 million people (SIAM). The challenge for Indian policymakers is to repeat the success achieved in the automobile sector in other manufacturing sectors.

Manufacturing is key to generating the jobs required to employ the 12 million new entrants to the labor market each year. While value-added services have provided 54 percent of India's GDP and especially the information-technology sector has contributed to 67 percent of India's services exports, Indian manufacturing has trailed not only that of East

Asian countries such as South Korea and Taiwan, but also of smaller economies like Vietnam and Bangladesh. As a percentage of GDP (16.5 percent), manufacturing in India has remained unchanged since the liberalization of economic activity in 1991. In comparison, manufacturing accounts for 29 percent of economic output in China and South Korea, and 27 percent in Thailand.

It is not surprising then that India plans to raise manufacturing as a percentage of GDP from 17 percent to 25 percent, and to create 100 million jobs within a decade. The 2014 National Manufacturing Policy (Make in India) addressed the areas of regulation, infrastructure, skills development, technology, availability of funding, exit mechanism etc. It is unlikely that India will be able to replicate the manufacturing success of its East Asian peers as its prospects will transect with global technological and economic trends. The rise of automation has raised questions about whether a focus on manufacturing can lead to a faster economic growth.

India has a revealed comparative advantage (RCA) only in a small number of manufacturing sub-sectors when compared to other emerging economies, according to the OECD data on trade in value-added. In addition, when a manufacturing sub-sector displays an RCA, it tends to be relatively small, as for example in the case of the production of textiles, textile products, leather and footwear. The main exception is the jewelry sector, where India has a significant RCA (Kaldor, 1967).

However, an IMF study (Thirlwall,1983) suggests that India has immense potential to diversify into products (emerging RCA) that are closely related to its current capabilities. In addition, it has good potential in expanding the exports to new areas, increasing the share of manufacturing in exports, increasing the sophistication of goods, and in improving the quality and complexity of exporting products. These products with emerging RCA belong to the 25 growth sectors as recognized by the *Make in India* initiative. *Make in India* took steps in the right direction by recognizing sectors with emerging comparative advantage.

Since the launch of *Make in India*, the country has improved its rank consistently and has seen a significant jump of 30 places in 2017 in the World Bank's annual ease of doing business survey (Figure 1) and has eased statutory restrictions on foreign direct investment across sectors (as measured by the OECD's FDI Regulatory Restrictiveness Index (Figure 2) where restrictions are evaluated on a 0 (open) to 1 (closed) scale).

Figure 1: Ease of doing business index

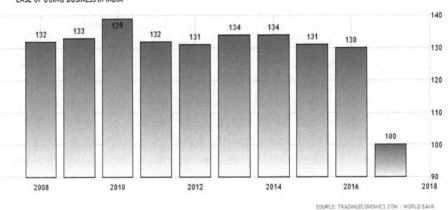

Figure 2: OECD FDI Regulatory Restrictiveness Index

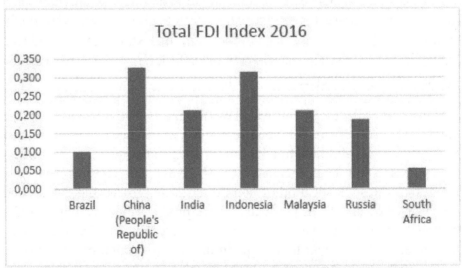

Source: OECD FDI Regulatory Restrictiveness Index – extracted 25 September 2017.

Current FDI policy in India is considered among the most liberal compared to other emerging economies. FDI of up to 100 percent is allowed under the automatic route in most sectors and activities. FDI inflows have grown by 15 percent between 2014-16 (Figure 3). In 2015, India surpassed China to become the top destination for FDI in Asia, attracting around US$63 billion investment flows. However, the number of greenfield FDI projects in India during 2017 fell sharply by 21% according to the 2018 FDI Report. China received foreign capital investment of $50.8 billion in 2017 in greenfield projects, where India attracted $25.1 billion.

Figure 3: FDI inflows to India (USD Millions)

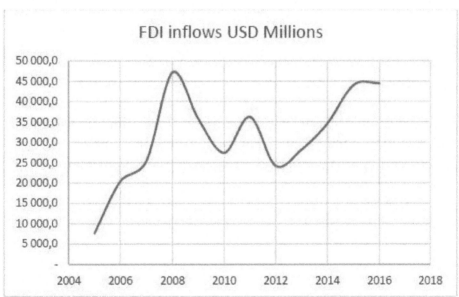

Source: UNCTAD, WIR 2017.

Although FDI inflows were on the rise between 2014-16, the declining investment to GDP ratio (Figure 4) suggests FDI flowing towards brownfield investments in the face of collapsing domestic private and public investment.

Figure 4: Investment (GFCF) as a percentage of GDP

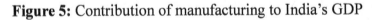

Source: OECD (2017)

Falling domestic investment has mirrored the decline in value-added manufacturing in India's GDP (Figure 5) (World Bank, 2008).

Figure 5: Contribution of manufacturing to India's GDP

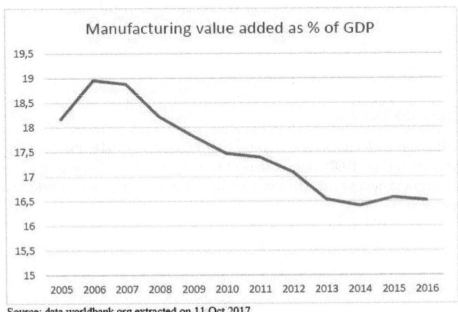

Source: data.worldbank.org extracted on 11 Oct 2017.

Figures on real gross value-added (GVA) for 2015-16 revealed that higher growth rates were spurred by strong industrial growth (Table 1). In 2015-16, growth in agriculture and related activities were estimated at just 1.2 percent while growth in the industrial and services sectors reached 7.4 and 8.9 percent respectively. The growth rate in manufacturing at 9.3 percent in 2015-16 was credited to the *Make in India* initiative.

Despite this sudden elevated growth rate in real GVA for the years 2015-16 (concerns have been raised that the new National Accounts Statistics (NAS) Series significantly over-states growth in manufacturing), there is no denying that the share of manufacturing in economic activity has revealed a downward trend since 2012-13.

Figures 6, 7 and 8 on IIP, India's manufacturing production and PMI demonstrate this declining trend.

Table 1: Real GVA growth in Indian manufacturing (%)

	2012-13	2013-14	2014-15	2015-16
Real GVA from the new NAS (base 2011-12)	6.0	5.6	5.5	9.3
Real GVA in manufacturing obtained from ASI data	6.5	2.0	NA	NA
Real GVA in private sector manufacturing companies covered in the RBI quarterly survey	1.7	0.9	3.3	9.7
Index of Industrial production, manufacturing	1.3	-0.8	2.3	2.0
Real GVA from the previous NAS series (base 2004-05)	1.1	-0.7		

Source: Goldar (2016)

Figure 6: Growth India industrial production index %
(covers mining, manufacturing and electricity)

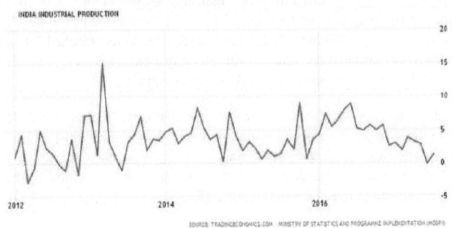

Figure 7: Growth in manufacturing production %

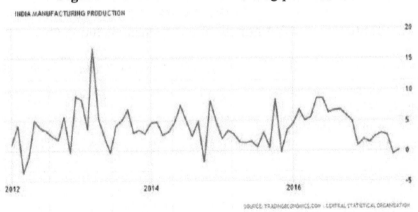

Figure 8: India Purchasing Manager's Index

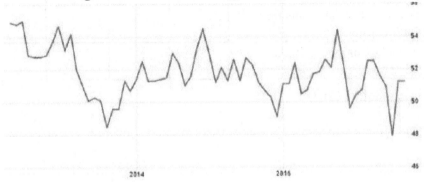

Source: Markit Economics

This downward trend has been manifested in exports of manufactured goods as well (Figure 9). India's exports which were sliding steadily since 2014, showed an increase of 4.7 percent in 2016-17. However, that increase has stalled.

Figure 9: India Volume of Exports in USD Million

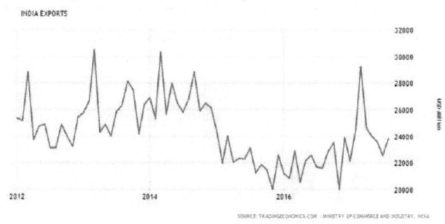

The current account after having declined consecutively for 4 years, has risen again in 2017 on the back of a higher imports manufacturing (Figure 10).

Figure 10: India's current account deficit as percentage of GDP

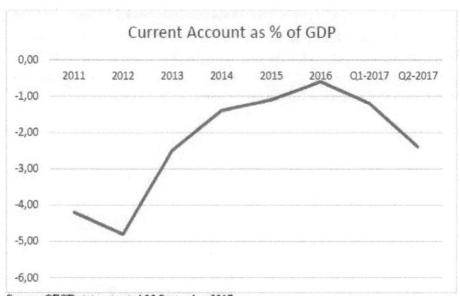

Source: OECD stat, extracted 25 September 2017.

The downward trend in many of the economic variables has been unambiguous since the beginning of 2017. The output growth has slowed to 5.7 percent against the backdrop of demonetization and introduction of the GST. Imports to India jumped by 21 percent compared to the previous year in August 2017. In April-August 2017-18, imports climbed to 26.6 percent over the same period of 2016 (Figure 11).

Figure 11: India's imports since demonetisation (USD Millions)

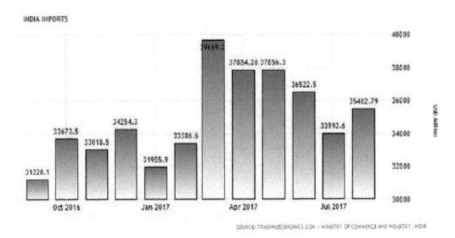

Stronger imports have affected GDP growth. Furthermore, as imports have surged, domestic production (IP, PMIs) has stumbled (Figures 12, 13). This suggests that domestic supply chains have potentially been disrupted in the manufacturing sector post-demonetization – likely to involve small and medium enterprises (SMEs) – and that activity has been replaced by imports, despite slowing domestic demand.

Figure 12: India's Index of Industrial Production 2016-17
(Oct 2016=100)

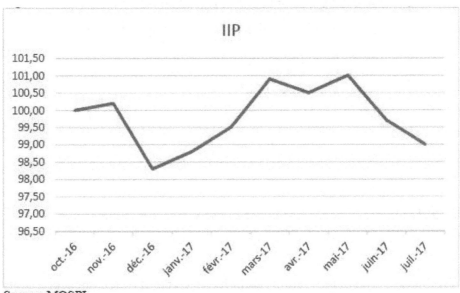

Source: MOSPI

Figure 13: Purchasing Manager's Index

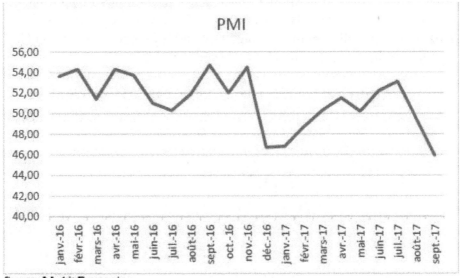

Source: Markit Economics

In addition, the economy has been suffering from the cumulative impact of an overvalued exchange rate that has adversely affected domestic production and has been sucking in imports (Figure 14).

Figure 14: India's real effective exchange rate (REER)

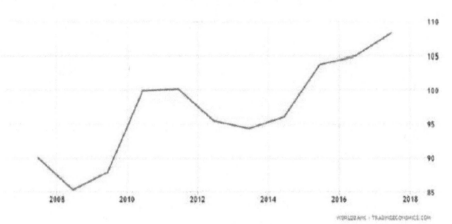

The introduction of GST in July 2017 has been beset by technical problems, undermining India's exports. Small and Medium Enterprises (SMEs) raised concerns about the compliance burden and difficulties in filing monthly returns while exporters have faced difficulties in securing tax refunds resulting in access to working capital (Wells & Thirlwall, 2003). This supply side disruption was inevitable after demonetization and GST, and the gap has been fulfilled by imports (Figure 15).

Figure 15: India volume of imports in USD Million

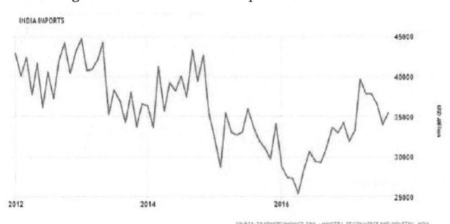

The challenge is in ensuring that this transitory phenomenon of increased imports does not become permanent. The cumulative effect of an overvalued currency, demonetization and the hurried implementation of GST may have exacerbated an enduring trend in the loss of India's competitiveness in production and exports of manufactured goods.

That loss of competitiveness in manufacturing is directly related to rigidity in the quality of, and access to, India's factor markets as well as several infrastructural and regulatory bottlenecks, resulting in considerable factor market misallocation and lower productivity.

CURRENT CHALLENGES FACING INDIA IN BECOMING A MANUFACTURING HUB

The success of the auto industry offers significant experience to Indian manufacturing, especially to advanced manufacturing sectors such as defense, aircraft, and ship building. The government has introduced significant policy changes to realize this objective and expand the experience of the auto industry. However, manufacturers still face significant hurdles. The majority of FDI, since *Make in India*'s inauguration, has been in the services sector, which attracted 60 percent of India's total FDI inflows from 2016 to 2017. Weak infrastructure has hindered the *Make in India* initiative. The futuristic *Smart Cities Mission*, set out to develop infrastructure, has not yet come to fruition in a way to stimulate growth in manufacturing. The requirements of high skilled people for the manufacturing sector are misaligned with the existing skill profile of India's young labor force. Regulations that have yet to be streamlined and a shallow supply chain ecosystem are additional challenges.

It is too early to call *Make in India* a success or a failure. Despite some significant policy changes, India still urgently needs to address a number of policy and practical implementation issues before investors shift their attention away from goods that are made in China for decades and towards 'Make in India'. The ten most important of these are discussed in detail below and include, *inter alia*:

* Reforming labor regulations to support enterprise growth
* Improving education and training
* Making land acquisition more efficient

- Reforming corporate and other taxation as it relates to manufacturing
- Making Bilateral Investment Treaties (BITs) more user friendly
- Improving and quickening regulatory approvals
- Removing infrastructure bottlenecks
- Dealing with high tariff and non-tariff barriers, and trade facilitation
- Dealing with the non-performing assets in public sector banks; and, finally
- Eliminating high levels of endemic corruption at central, state and local levels of government which continue to persist despite an ostensible anti-corruption stance.

Reforming labor regulations to support enterprise growth: Among reforms in factor markets, reforming labor laws is crucial for creating more jobs. Despite an abundance in unskilled labor, Indian firms have expanded largely in capital-intensive sectors (engineering goods, pharmaceuticals) or used excessively capital-intensive technologies in other sectors, resulting in low utilization of labor.

Labor laws which make firing (and therefore hiring) difficult also introduce other rigidities leading to increase in the cost of labor, thus incentivizing deployment of highly capital-intensive technologies. Regulating companies' ability to fire factory workers, especially for larger companies, led to many factories staying small to avoid increased regulatory burdens, while many others try to have their records show their workers as contract labor.

Labor market rigidities remain high because of the multiplicity of labor laws and high costs of meeting legal requirements. The Industrial Disputes Act (IDA) of 1947 is the basis of industrial labor regulations in India (it requires firms employing 100 workers or more to seek government's permission to dismiss a worker or to close a plant); firms are required to comply with numerous, complex and ambiguous laws governing different aspects of the labor market (such as laws governing minimum wages, resolution of industrial disputes, conditions for hiring and firing workers, and conditions for the closure of establishments etc.).

Labor market rigidities have resulted in a large informal (unorganized) sector which employs nearly 90 percent of the Indian workforce. Although the informal sector provides useful employment opportunities, the persistent high level of informality has failed to improve labor welfare (as workers operate in an unregulated environment, are paid low wages with no job security), negating the very motive of India's pro-worker regulations. The government has simplified administration of labor laws through an online portal called Shram Suvidha.

Although several initiatives have been taken at central and state government levels to reduce the detrimental effects of India's onerous and rigid labor regulations, significant reforms are needed to promote quality employment and reduce income inequality. These regulations protect the formal sector while increasing the size of the informal sector that evades them.

Reform of labor regulations should aim at providing a minimum floor of pay as well as adequate social and labor protection for all workers, irrespective of the status, size and activity of any firm. This would require introducing a comprehensive labor law which would consolidate and simplify existing regulations and reduce uncertainty surrounding regulations as well as compliance costs for companies. Legislative changes to bring about some significant labor reforms, like simplification of labor laws reducing the 44 labor laws into 4 codes, have been delayed. In the meantime, the responsibility for introducing labor reforms has been delegated to state governments.

Improving education and training: The average age of India's population by 2020 is projected to be the lowest in the world— around 29 whereas it is 37 in China and the United States of America, 45 in West Europe, and 48 in Japan. While the global economy is expected to witness a shortage in the young population by 2020 with around 56 million, India will be the only country with a youth surplus of 47 million.

India's demographic transition makes it imperative to ensure employment opportunities for millions of youth each year. Alongside employment, skill development is equally important as over the years jobs have become more skill-intensive with changes in technology as well as increased inter-linkages across economic activities.

India needs to equip 15 million people by 2020 with the skills necessary to realize Make in India's aim to bring more high-grade manufacturing to the country. The country, however, faces a big challenge ahead. It is estimated (per the latest survey by the Labor Bureau for 2013-14) that only 4.69 percent of persons aged 15 years and above have received or were receiving vocational training, of which only 2.8 percent was through formal channels while 4 percent was through the informal system (Szirmai & Bart, 2015).

The skill development issue in India is pertinent both at the demand and supply level. Generating employment is a challenge given the enormity of population entering the workforce each year. From the supply side, the issue is primarily related to employability of the workforce due to varying reasons ranging from poor education, lack of training facilities, inadequate skilling, quality issues leading to the mismatch of skill requirements, and poor perception of vocational skilling vis-à-vis formal education.

Aspiring Minds, an Indian employability assessment firm, has suggested in its 2016 report that more than 80 percent of engineers in India are "unemployable," after a study of about 150,000 engineering students in around 650 engineering colleges in the country. Workers trained in the vocational education and training system often require significant on-the-job training.

Given the lack of access to education and quality of education, continuing to improve access to education, especially at the secondary level, and improving the quality of education is imperative. As a step to raising quality, monitoring learning outcomes, tracking implementation and follow-up in monitoring the reforms is essential. India should collaborate closely with employers when designing vocational education and training programs to ensure that they are relevant to labor market needs.

Making land acquisition more efficient: India's new land law was designed to resolve one of the most vexing problems of state acquisition of agricultural land for industry, infrastructure and urban development. India's previous 1894 land acquisition law gave the state unchecked powers to take private land for projects deemed of public interest, including private investments. Private companies have mostly relied on state procured land for big projects. However, these powers were widely abused, with farmers coerced into relinquishing land at throwaway prices usually to see the land resold afterwards for far more; with middlemen (usually local and state-level politicians) reaping windfall profits. This exploitation, and lack of alternative livelihoods, led to fierce resistance.

To address the land acquisition issue, Parliament passed the Right to Fair Compensation and Transparency in Land Acquisition, Rehabilitation and Resettlement Bill in 2013. It took effect in 2014, offering a fairer, more transparent process that protects the interests of land sellers and land seekers, thus facilitating land acquisition deals. While the new Land Acquisition Bill will increase the direct cost of land acquisition, it is also expected to reduce the indirect costs as the incidence of disputes and litigation should decline.

Still, the process of acquiring land may be long and fraught. Land ownership still remains opaque, and re-zoning, from agricultural to industrial zones, has been fraught with risks and delays. Implementation of the law in practice needs to be more flexible and closely monitored; the weaknesses should be amended as needed. The government urgently needs to review the timelines established by the Bill and aim to make land acquisition faster. The institutional set-up should allow for swift resolution of disputes.

The government introduced nine main amendments to the 2013 legislation through an ordinance in 2014, and subsequently as part of an amendment Bill in 2015. However, due to stiff opposition from various political parties, the government agreed to drop most of its amendments and reintroduced clauses related to consent of affected families and social impact assessments. Other amendments are now under the consideration of a joint parliamentary committee.

Reforming taxation: The World Bank ranks India 172nd out of 190 countries in 2017 in the "Ease of Paying Taxes". The overall effective tax rate for small to medium sized companies is relatively high. The indirect tax system is complex, costly to comply with and puts India's manufacturing sector at a competitive disadvantage in international markets.

The Goods and Services Tax (GST) which was introduced in July 2017, is expected to result in the dismantling of inter-state check posts, and to improve the domestic and international competitiveness of Indian manufacturing firms significantly. Simply halving the delays due to road blocks, tolls and other stoppages could cut freight times by 20-30 percent and logistics costs by an even higher amount, 30-40 percent. This alone can go a long way in boosting the competitiveness of India's key manufacturing sectors by 3 to 4 percent of net sales, thereby helping India return to a high growth path and enabling large scale job creation.

State border check-points, tasked primarily with carrying out compliance procedures for the diverse sales and entry tax requirements of different states, combined with other delays, keep trucks from moving during 60 percent of the entire end-to-end transit time. High variability and unpredictability in shipments add to total logistics costs in the form of higher-than-optimal buffer stocks and lost sales, pushing logistics costs in India 2-3 times more than those of international benchmarks (Chakravarty & Mitra, 2009).

The corporate income tax (CIT) system in India is characterized by high effective tax rates and a narrow tax base. High effective tax rates result from the imposition of several charges on top of an already significant statutory CIT rate, together with a corporate-level tax on distributed dividends (the dividend distribution tax). Even after the proposed reduction in the statutory CIT rate, effective tax rates for equity-financed investment will remain high, discouraging such investment. For example, average effective tax rates for an equity-financed investment range from 37.8 percent to 44.8 percent depending on asset type, while marginal effective tax rates range from 24.3 percent to 52.7 percent (Kathuria,& Rajesh, 2013).

The corporate tax base is narrow due to a wide range of tax concessions, while multinational enterprises are also able to minimize their tax liability in India by exploiting mismatches in international tax rules. These concessions result in some corporations paying significantly less tax than the high effective tax rates imply (Baumol, 1967).

Total gross corporate income tax concessions are estimated at INR 984 billion (Rodrik, 2016). This equates to 21.8 percent of CIT revenue (0.8 percent of GDP) in 2014-15. In addition to the loss in tax revenue, the effectiveness of such concessions in achieving their policy goals is often mixed and the concessions are relatively complex leading to costly disputes over eligibility, facilitating outright abuse. The overall business tax base is narrowed by a high degree of informality amongst small businesses.

To reduce the relatively high statutory CIT rate and broaden the narrow corporate tax base as compared to other major economies, the government announced in its 2015 budget that it would undertake CIT reform. Over four years from 2016, the government has proposed to reduce the statutory CIT rate (for resident corporations) from 30 percent to 25 percent. In addition, the government has proposed "rationalization and removal of various kinds of tax exemptions".

Meanwhile, apart from the complexity of the Indian tax system which complicates its interpretation and leaves too much to official discretion, an aggressive audit process and frequent changes in tax laws with retrospective effect have also undermined economic activity and resulted in India leading the world in numbers of tax disputes (OECD, 2014).

CBDT data show that in 2012-13, India had over 381,000 tax disputes. In particular, the implementation of retrospective legislation on the taxation of indirect transfers of assets, and tax administration rulings regarding the application of MAT (minimum alternative tax) to foreign institutional investors have been particularly damaging.

However, the recent introduction of an advance pricing agreement (APA) regime has increased business certainty for multinationals. The Easwar Committee was set up in 2015 to identify parts of the Income Tax Act that are unclear and lead to unnecessary disputes. It reported its findings in early 2016 and the government is currently considering its recommendations. Nevertheless, issues remain regarding the audit processes and transfer pricing rules (Anand, Kalpana & Saurabh, 2015).

Bilateral Investment Treaties (BITs): Since 1994, India had signed 84 BITs with countries such as the UK, France, Germany, Australia, China, Malaysia, Thailand, Mexico, Russia, Egypt, Saudi Arabia, the UAE, Turkey and others. Many of these BITs contained protection for investors (including commitments to fair and equitable treatment (FET), non-discrimination and most favored nation treatment (MFN), the ability to repatriate proceeds, and protection from expropriation. They also allowed for arbitration of alleged breaches of these protections directly between the investor and the host government.

However, in recent years, India has been facing several arbitration claims from investors under its BITs. This began with India losing a claim in 2011 that was brought by Australia alleging excessive judicial delays in enforcing a commercial arbitration award through the Indian courts. Further claims have since been brought on retrospective taxation, the allocation of satellite spectrum. In 2016, India was one of the most frequently-named respondent states in BIT proceedings (Mehrotra, 2017).

In early 2017, the government terminated bilateral investment treaties with 58 countries, including 22 EU countries. Many of these BITs ceased to apply to new investments from April 2017. For the remaining 26 of its BITs that have not completed their initial term, there is a proposed joint interpretative statement to the counterparties to align the ongoing treaties with the 2015 Model BIT. On the other hand, investments made before the termination of the 58 treaties may be protected for some years under the 'sunset' clauses in those BITs.

The new Model BIT contains more restrictive definitions of 'investor' and 'investment' and is intended to reduce the exposure of the Indian government to future claims, by excluding taxation measures from its domain and removing or qualifying the MFN and FET protections. The 2015 Model BIT preserves the mechanism for settlement of investor-state disputes by arbitration.

Until new arrangements are agreed between India and relevant counterparty states, new investments of foreign investors to be made in India and Indian investments to be made in the counterparty country will cease to receive BIT protections. The termination of BITs has sent mixed messages at a time when the government is taking vital steps to attract inbound investment through Make in India and when the outbound investment by Indian companies continues to increase in both developed and developing economies (Goldar, 2016).

Regulatory Approvals: Foreign investment in India has always been heavily regulated, requiring approvals from various government ministries. As a result, the Foreign Investment Promotion Board (FIPB) was established in August 1991. Regulatory approvals have caused substantial delays in project implementation. There were multiple agencies involved and various approvals were required across different stages of the project cycle. Many of the guidelines evolved continuously (often whimsically) and are needed to be implemented, not only in new projects, but also in under-construction projects, which then had to comply with revised standards midway through their execution stage. Several approvals did not have defined timelines.

In 2017, the government decided to get away with the FIPB. Now, foreign investment in any of the 11 notified sectors requires approval only from the concerned administrative ministry. The Department of Industrial Policy and Promotion has issued a Standard Operating Procedure (SoP) for processing FDI proposals under this new regime. The most significant feature of this SoP is the time period of 8-10 weeks within which investment applications are required to be cleared by the ministries concerned.

However, there are fundamental problems in the current Indian legal institutional framework around FDI approvals. the primary law concerning foreign investment – the Foreign Exchange Management Act, 1999 (FEMA) – does not create any institutional accountability. It does not prescribe any time limits for the finance ministry to clear foreign investment applications. FEMA does not clarify the purpose of government approval itself. Further, the law does not require the government to give any reasons for rejecting an investment application.

The DIPP's new SoP does not resolve any of these fundamental issues. The timelines it imposes on the ministries for various actions are not binding. The SoP does not change the internal incentive structure of the bureaucracy to ensure that they comply with the timelines, leading to a lack of time-bound inter-ministerial coordination needed for the grant of approvals (the Goods and Service Tax Council (GST), 2017).

The OECD Product Market Regulation Index (PMR) (Figure 16) measures the extent of a growth enhancing competitive environment in a country and a level playing field among firms. The aggregate PMR indicator is the simple average across three indicators that are state control, barriers to entrepreneurship and barriers to trade and investment. OECD estimates suggest that reducing India's score on the OECD's product market regulation indicator by 20 percent could boost the level of productivity by around 2 percent over the next 5 years (FICCI & Konrad, 2015) (World Bank, 2014).

Figure 16: OECD Product Market Regulation Index

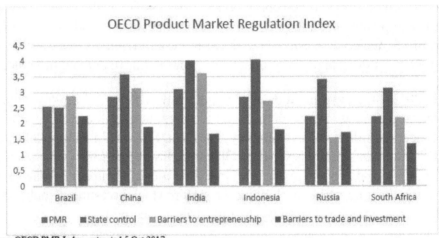

Source: OECD PMR Index, extracted 5 Oct 2017.

Infrastructure bottlenecks: In the last 20 years, although not as much as China, India has made substantial investments in infrastructure. In many areas, the investment and maintenance targets have not been met, leaving infrastructure in very poor condition. Firms in India face frequent power outages and transport infrastructure is below par.

Major new infrastructure investments are required because logistical bottlenecks need to be removed to lower the cost of doing business in India. The approach document for the 12th Five Year Plan (2012-17) projected a requirement of US$ 1 trillion for India's infrastructure development. Yet, infrastructure investment in India has been held back by poor governance, political challenges, lack of transparency in PPP bidding and awarding processes, delays in regulatory approvals and land clearances, lack of availability of long term debt, taxation issues (provisions to tax indirect investments) and lack of independent regulatory authorities in each of the infrastructure sectors.

Infrastructure bottlenecks have contributed to longer lead times and excess inventory having to be held across the value chain. Poor supply chain performance and reliability is one of the reasons why many foreign companies use their Indian factories mainly to serve the domestic market and avoid integrating them into their global networks.

Lack of investment in physical infrastructure has hampered integration not just domestically (connecting more remote regions), but also regionally and internationally. Investment in the maintenance and upgrading of existing and new infrastructure could provide an important boost to economic activity.

Beyond connectivity issues, India faces the critical challenge of power shortages (Thomas, 2017), which impedes the smooth functioning of GVCs. Electricity supply in India is seen to be on par with Cambodia, the worst performer in SEA. In terms of logistics performance, India's performance stands between that of Thailand and Indonesia (OECD, 2017).

The government has taken several steps to promote the flow of long-term funds into infrastructure investment e.g. setting up Infrastructure Debt Funds, raising foreign institutional investor (FII) limits for infrastructure, and liberalizing external commercial borrowing (ECB) limits. India has also attracted private capital in recent years. Deepening bond markets by gradually relaxing the restrictions on domestic and foreign investors would expand financing.

High tariff and non-tariff barriers, trade facilitation: High import tariffs and non-tariff barriers also hinder the productivity and competitiveness of the manufacturing sector. Tariffs have been cut significantly since the early 1990s, yet tariffs remain high compared to other BRICs and OECD countries. India also imposes non-tariff barriers in the form of quantitative restrictions, import licensing, burdensome mandatory testing and certification for a large number of products.

In terms of trade facilitation, the World Bank (2010) has noted that for Nepal to trade goods with India, it takes around 200 signatures; while trading from India to Nepal requires around 140. At one important border between Bangladesh and India, trucks are often required to wait over four days in order to cross the border.

The OECD Trade Facilitation Indicators suggest that India performs better than the averages of Asian and lower-middle income countries in a number of areas including information availability, involvement of the trade community, advance rulings, appeal procedures and fees and charges (Figure 17). However, India could draw considerable benefits in terms of trade volumes and trade costs by streamlining border procedures.

Trade facilitation and better infrastructure are necessary, but are insufficient conditions for further value chain participation. These measures need to be complemented with MFN tariff liberalization and institutional reform. Efforts to this end could help attract foreign investment in new technologies complementary to India's labor abundance. In many respects, and particularly in terms of labor endowments, India resembles many South East Asian countries, and therefore should be able to attract important GVC activity, which may help further regional development objectives (MAT, 2014/2015).

Figure 17: OECD Trace Facilitation Indicators

Source: OECD, extracted 4 Oct 2017.
Note: The TFIs take values from 0 to 2, where 2 represents the best performance that can be achieved.

Non-performing assets in public sector banks: Corporate and banking sector vulnerabilities have had serious implications on the overall investment environment of the country. According to the 2016-17 Economic Survey, 57 percent of the top stressed debtors would require to reduce their debt levels by 75 percent to restore viability, suggesting that there is little capacity to raise funding for capital expenditure or to attract investors to turn the assets around.

The NPA problem of public sector banks is a deep structural sign of crony capitalism. To deal with the NPA problem the government has reformed insolvency laws by enacting the Insolvency and Bankruptcy Code in 2016 and made it operational soon. Until the Code, there was no single legislation that governed corporate insolvency and bankruptcy proceedings in India. The government has empowered the Reserve Bank of India (RBI) to force banks to resolve and restructure stressed assets by invoking the bankruptcy code against defaulters. The government has also consolidated one bank—the State Bank. However, these measures have failed to provide a comprehensive strategy of how the public sector banking can return to sustainability.

Moreover, in October 2017, the government agreed to recapitalize public sector banks by Rs. 2.11 trillion (equivalent to about 1.3 percent of GDP) between 2017-19 as banks undergo the resolution process through the new bankruptcy law. What is different about this recapitalization is that the government will issue Rs. 1.35 trillion as "recapitalization bonds" over the next two years. Along with this, recent steps to overhaul the bankruptcy laws have finally drawn a line under delinquent loans. It is expected that during 2018-19, the assets and debts of about 50 largest defaulters may be sold off by court-appointed professionals, in a process in which banks are likely to face losses of up to 60 percent on their loans.

Public sector banks have been used by political parties over the years to sustain political corruption and to implement government policies. The fight against corruption will be incomplete if it does not include policies to tackle the issues of corporate governance in public sector banks.

Corruption: India has been overwhelmed by endemic corruption in recent times. According to Transparency International's 2016 Corruption Perception Index, India ranks 79th, tied with China, among 176 countries. Corruption has acted as a non-transparent tax on India's growth leading to higher costs and delays. Corruption is especially prevalent in the judiciary, police, tax, public services and public procurement sectors.

Due to varying levels of corruption and the poor quality of government operations across India, local investment conditions vary between and within states. The Prevention of Corruption Act is the principal legal framework that focuses on corruption in the public sector. Both active and passive bribery are covered by this legislation, and public officials are only allowed to accept gifts of nominal value.

Due to low levels of enforcement and monitoring however, integrity in state bodies is lacking, and corrupt practices such as facilitation payments and bribes persist. Significant reasons most frequently put forward for the level of corruption in India are its public and corporate governance regimes. The new Companies Act, enacted in 2013, is seen as important in improving the ease and efficiency of doing business in India. It deals with strengthening of the internal controls through corporate governance, corporate social responsibility, auditor rotation, and investor protection.

The New Act holds out the possibility of reducing the risk of corrupt practices. Despite the government has stepped up its efforts to counter corruption, red tape and bribery continue to be widespread.

CONCLUSION
Manufacturing has the potential to lift half a billion more of India's population out of poverty through income, export and employment growth. However, the contribution of manufacturing in India's economic activity has been declining steadily for the last ten years. Recently, demonetization, technical problems associated with the introduction of GST and an overvalued currency, have exacerbated an enduring trend in the loss of India's competitiveness in the production and the exports of manufactured goods.

Structural bottlenecks have long affected the manufacturing sector, more than the services sector. India's failure to industrialize is due to labor market legislation which puts a tariff on large-scale manufacturing establishments and the long and fraught process to acquire land for industrial or infrastructure projects. Firms often cannot find employees with the right skills and training. Power outages and poor infrastructure also make it difficult for firms to be competitive and reach new markets.

If India was successful in unlocking its factor markets, especially land and labor for manufacturing, domestic and global corporations will accelerate the transformation. Unfortunately, the half measures taken to unlock land and labor have included passing the responsibility to regional governments, anticipating strong resistance from trade unions and caste lobbies.

In 2015, the government failed to repeal and replace the Land Acquisition Act of the previous government. That experience early in its term has resulted in the government proceeding cautiously in getting vital legislation passed. Despite the frequent assertion of nationalism, decisions on rational economic policies give precedence to the most divisive local interests, show weakness in face of mass defiance and show the government's inability to break the trade-off between alleviating a problem and tackling it.

Despite the government's inclination, the introduction of the GST is a significant reform which establishes a single market in goods and services with a uniform indirect tax structure. The fact that it has taken 15 years to pass the legislation on GST is an indictment of India's corrosive politics. However, GST was compromised by poor design and implementation; with far too many rates over-complicating the regime, creating goods classification problems and imposing administrative burdens. The teething problems are much larger and therefore will take much longer to resolve.

There is no disagreement over why India has been steadily losing its competitiveness in manufacturing. Addressing structural bottlenecks, in particular rigid labor laws, inadequate investment in human capital, difficult process of land acquisition, regulation, and access to funding has been constrained by India's political compunctions.

Consequently, the progress that India has made in driving forward its *Make in India* initiative is confined largely to processes related to the ease of doing business, trade facilitation, and easing statutory restrictions on foreign direct investment across sectors.

For the *Make in India* initiative to have any realistic chance of any significant success, India urgently needs to address its more fundamental structural bottlenecks. Notwithstanding the dynamic marketing and exhortative campaigns for driving the *Make in India* initiative, achieving its objectives has remained daunting from the outset. It will continue to be challenging, given the serious structural and policy-reform deficits that remain to be addressed. In addition, the campaign – which relies too heavily on marketing and not enough on policy-product development -- has created expectations that cannot be met easily.

REFERENCES

[1] With $2.3 trillion in GDP, India is the world's ninth-largest economy and the third largest by purchasing power parity at $8 trillion (World Bank).

[2] ILO (2016). 'India Labor Market Update.' ILO Country Office for India.

[3] Dhawan, Rajat, Gautam Swaroop, and Adil Zainulbhai (2012). Fulfilling the promise of India's manufacturing sector. McKinsey and Company.

[4] Kaldor, N. 1967.Strategic Factors in Economic Development. Ithaca, NY: Cornell University.

[5] Thirlwall A.P. 1983. A Plain Man's Guide to Kaldor's Growth Laws. *Journal of Post Keynesian Economics* 5: 345–358.

[6] World Bank, Commission on Growth and Development. 2008. *The growth report: strategies for sustained growth and inclusive development.*

[7] Dasgupta S. & Singh A. 2005. Will Services be the New Engine of Indian Economic Growth? *Development and Change* 36: 1035–57.

[8] Wells H. & Thirlwall A.P. 2003. Testing Kaldor's Growth Laws across the Countries of Africa. *African Development Review* 15: 89–105.

[9] Szirmai, Adam and Bart Verspagen. 2015. "Manufacturing and Economic Growth in Developing Countries, 1950-2005." Structural Change and Economic Dynamics 34: 46-59.

[10] Chakravarty, S. and A. Mitra (2009), Is Industry still the engine of growth? An econometric study of the organized sector employment in India, Journal *of Policy Modeling* 31, 22-35.

[11] Kathuria, Vinish and Rajesh R. Natarajan. 2013. "Is Manufacturing an Engine of Growth in India in the Post-Nineties?" Journal of South Asian Development 8(3): 385-408.

[12] Baumol, William J. 1967. "Macroeconomics of Unbalanced Growth: The Anatomy of Urban Crisis." *American Economic Review* 57 (3): 415–26.

[13] Rodrik, Dani. 2016. "Premature Deindustrialization." *Journal of Economic Growth* 21: 1–33.

[14] OECD (2014a). Economic Survey of India.

[15] Anand, Rahul, Kalpana Kochhar and Saurabh Mishra (2015), "Make in India: Which Exports Can Drive the Next Wave of Growth?" IMF Working Paper No. 15/119

[16] Excessive imports have affected Indian manufacturing for the last 12-15 years. This is due to higher duties on intermediate goods compared to final finished goods, with the latter often enjoying concessional customs duty. This inverted duty structure has resulted in higher raw material cost at home. FICCI has pointed in a 2014 study the issue of inverted duties for sectors like aluminium, steel, chemicals, capital goods, electronics (Mehrotra, 2017).

[17] Goldar, Bishwanath (2016). Manufacturing growth in India in recent years: Is it getting overstated in India's new GDP series? Indian Growth and Development Review, 9 (2), 102-113.

[18] In response to the difficulties faced by the SMEs and exporters, the Goods and Service Tax (GST) Council in October 2017 introduced measures to ease the compliance burden of SMEs and access to funding for exporters.

[19] FICCI and Konrad Adenauer Stiftung (2015). Skills development in India.

[20] World Bank (2014). India development update.

[21] Thomas et al. (2017). Taxation and investment in India. OECD Economics Department Working Papers, No. 1397.

[22] OECD (2017). Economic Survey of India.

[23] The minimum alternate tax (MAT) was estimated to claw back INR 360 billion in 2014-15, reducing the total revenue forgone to INR 624 billion.

[24] OECD (2017). Economic Survey of India.

[25] Ibid.

[26] Peacock and Joseph (2017). Mixed messages to investors as India quietly terminates bilateral investment treaties with 58 countries. Herbert Smith Freehills Arbitration notes.

[27] Ibid.

[28] Datta, Pratik, Radhika Pandey and Sumant Prashant (2017). Replacing FIPB with Standard Operating Procedure not enough. https://ajayshahblog.blogspot.fr

[29] OECD (2014b). Improving the business environment through effective regulation. OECD India Policy Brief.

[30] Koske, I., I. Wanner, R. Bitetti and O. Barbiero (2015). The 2013 update of the OECD product market regulation indicators: policy insights for OECD and non-OECD countries. OECD Economics Department Working Papers, No. 1200.

[31] Ahmed, S., S. Kelegama and E. Ghani (eds.) (2010). Promoting Economic Cooperation in South Asia. World Bank.

[32] OECD (2015). The Participation of Developing Countries in Global Value Chains: Implications for Trade and Trade-Related Policies.

[33] Ibid.

China's Outward Foreign Direct Investment Along "Belt and Road Initiative"

Sedat AYBAR[1]
Meryem GÜREL[2]

Abstract

This article examines the motivations and determinants of China's Outward Foreign Direct Investment (OFDI) within the new lands called The Belt and Road Initiative (BRI) inspired by the ancient Silk Road. Although China's OFDI has always been important for academic interest, OFDI along the BRI is a distinctive economic policy for China at the global stage. The existing literature demonstrates that China's OFDI with its economic policy is based on its national modernization. As China's multivariate domestic economy requires different strategies with diversified outward investments along the BRI and non-BRI countries, it has positive return to the country. The investigation hereby indicates that China's OFDI has different motivations for natural resources, strategic assets, market and efficiency seeking. Its determinants are cost advantage, institutions, market size, national agglomeration, cultural proximity, free trade agreement (FTA) expanding trade relations and qualified labor in low-income and middle-income countries. The transfer of CO_2 emissions requiring industrial selection is also a driver of China's OFDI aiming the reduction of air pollution for climate change. Besides the efforts of China, the state-owned enterprises need reforms to broaden ownership for further outward investments as an implication.

Keywords: *China, OFDI, Belt and Road Initiative, Chinese SOEs*

[1] Professor and the Head of Department of Economics and Finance and The Director of China Study Centre at İstanbul Aydın University
[2] Graduate Student in International Economy, Department of Economics and Finance, İstanbul Aydın University

INTRODUCTION

China has a remarkable 35 years of economic development marked by an achievement of becoming a middle-income country from a merely $190 to over $10,000 per capita income at the present. Inward foreign direct investment (IFDI) has a major role in China's economic growth accompanying a process of trade diversification and building up large USD reserve holdings. Despite such economic growth, unequal income distribution, particula,rly after the slump of the global economy in 2008, brought forward the discussion about the need for China's economic modernization. Not only unsustainable macroeconomic conditions, but also the discordance between government policy and market liberalization, poor institutions, corruption, manufacturing and export led economy were some of the challenges that needed to be reckoned in China.

China's transition from a market-based economy to a services-based economy required a set of new reforms to readjust country's IFDI aligned with China's outward foreign direct investment (OFDI) as "Going Out" strategy. President Xi Jinping unveiled a visionary policy called The Belt and Road Initiative (BRI) with outward investments in the lead to rebuild landlocked regions with regards to its national modernization as a part of "going out" strategy. Although the BRI is a new issue and has a vague data, China's OFDI has always been important for academic interest and its OFDI along the BRI is a unique and a distinctive economic policy for China at the global stage. Analyzing the existing literature of motivations and determinants of China's OFDI constitutes the aim of this article.

Drawing upon the existing literature, China's going out strategy is based on its national modernization. China's transition to services-trade economy is to rebalance the national income by readjusting FDI policy among domestic and cross-borders arenas. The main purpose of this study is to discover the motivations and determinants of China's OFDI along the BRI despite the BRI having no clear data. While China's FDI has always been in academic interest, China's OFDI along the BRI is a new issue for academic researches.

The rest of the article is structured as follows, the mega projects along the BRI is investigated in the next i.e. second section, patterns of Chinese Outward Foreign Direct Investment is studied in the third section. Fourth section focuses on the strategies of Chinese state-owned enterprises (SOEs) and the following section concludes.

MEGA PROJECTS ALONG THE BELT AND ROAD INITIATIVE

- **The Belt and Road Initiative**

China's visionary President Xi Jinping declared that China had a significant universe to integrate with the global economy in terms of Outward Foreign Direct Investment (OFDI) with a concrete strategy called The Belt and Road Initiative (BRI) that aims to build two routes, namely Silk Road Economic Belt (SREB) in 2013 and Maritime Silk Road (MSR) in 2014. The BRI covers 65 countries on three continents Asia, Europe and Africa aiming a win-win cooperation by advancing the priorities with five main purpose; policy coordination, infrastructure, reducing trade barriers, financial integration and people to people connectivity (Xinhuanet, 2015).

The Silk Road Economic Belt (SREB) connects from Xi'an in China passing through the inland region through Khorgas-Central Asia to Middle East, Turkey combining Asia to East Europe reaching to Rotterdam Holland. The Marietime Silk Road (MSR) starts from the east coast state Fujian in China opening to South China Sea passing through Malacca Strait to Indian Ocean reaching to Mediterranean Sea via Gulf of Aden and Red Sea from Athens-Greece ending in Venice-Italy with three prominent oil-transit straits (Tiezzi 2015). Mega projects were designed to build a multilayered geographical connectivity with diversified investments particularly infrastructure investments such as highways, roads, railways, ports, airports, construction, telecommunication, energy being financed by Asian Infrastructure and Investment Bank (AIIB) which 57 member countries signed multilateral agreement as the financial architect of BRI. Although there has been 1700 agreed BRI projects, the BRI data is not clear (Huang 2017).

65 Countries along The Belt and Road	
Region	**Countries**
East Asia	China, Mongolia
Southeast Asia	Brunei, Cambodia, Indonesia, Laos, Malaysia, Myanmar, Philippines, Singapore, Timor-Leste, Thailand, Vietnam
South Asia	Afghanistan, Bangladesh, Bhutan, India, Maldives, Nepal, Pakistan, Sri Lanka
Central Asia	Kazakhstan, Kyrgzstan, Tajikistan, Turkmenistan, Uzbekistan
Middle East & North Africa	Bahrain, Egypt, Iran, Iraq, Israel, Jordan, Kuwait, Lebanon, Oman, Palestine, Qatar, Saudi Arabia, Syria, United Arab Emirates, Yemen,
Europe	Albania, Armenia, Azerbaijan, Belarus, Bosnia & Herzegovina, Bulgaria, Czech Republic, Croatia, Estonia, Georgia, Hungary, Latvia, Lithuania, Macedonia, Moldova, Montenegro, Poland, Romania, Russia, Serbia, Slovakia, Slovenia, Turkey, Ukraine

Source: (2016) The Belt and Road Initiative: 65 Countries and Beyond, Fung Business Intelligence Centre

The multilayered connectivity is designed through six economic corridors to achieve SREB and MSR, these are: i) The New Eurasia Land Bridge Economic Corridor starts in the province of Jiangsu-China going through inland region Xinjiang on Central Asia reaching to Germany-Europe over Russia. ii) The second one is the China-Mongolia-Russia Economic Corridor bridging Eurasia. iii) The third one is the China-Central Asia-West Asia Economic Corridor starting from Xinjiang through railways to Central Asia and West Asia reaching to Mediterranean coast and the Arabian Peninsula. iv) The fourth one is China and Indochina Peninsula Economic Corridor, which is a particular region on Southeast Asia planned as a transportation network, industrial projects and fundraise for a sustainable socio-economic development. v) The fifth one is China-Pakistan Economic Corridor starting from Kashgar-Xinjiang going down to Gwadar coast in the city of Balochistan in Pakistan, which is an important transferring port for Chinese Shipping. Two countries cooperated to advance the Karakoram Highway which is an expressway at the east of the bay of Gwadar Port, a new international airport, an expressway from Karachi to Lahore, the Lahore rail transport orange line, the Haier-Ruba economic zone, and China-Pakistan cross-national optic fiber network. vi) The sixth one is the Bangladesh-China-India-Myanmar Economic Corridor aiming to expand investment and trade relations by building infrastructures (HKTDC 2017).

- **Investment Projects**

After Cold War and economic crisis in the new century, the trends of investments have required long term, high and risky-payments, transparency and accountability and a good financial management. The cross-border production characterized with zone, scale and know-how which meant strategic trade can no longer be operated by trial and learning or traditional management but professional management with western multinational enterprises (MNEs) (Moran, 1999). As a result of the rise of third world countries, trends of FDI has changed. China has impact on developing countries as new coming FDI policy in the new century as four types of FDI in extractive, infrastructure, manufacturing and assembly services based on research. Each of them has idiosyncratic challenges and opportunities as well as policies of its own (Moran, 2011a).

The rising production of export-based Chinese economy increased its supply-side i.e. need of oil, energy and raw materials. Today, China is the world's largest consumer and exporter of Rare-Earth Elements (REE) for innovative production and developing technologies (Moran, 2011b). China is one of the largest investors in Africa with US$ 36 billion capital investment and has 88 projects in 37 African countries in the fields of real estate, infrastructure, manufacturing, mining and energy to boost trade relations. Due to construction of highways, ports and airports, not only oil and energy demand is increasing but also heavy vehicles. China Petroleum

Pipeline is the leading company in terms of employment with two pipeline projects invested in Mozambique and South Africa in order to transport natural gas. The recovery of African economy accelerated the investments from China and led Chinese investors diversifying their interest to renewable energies rather than conventional sectors (Klasa, 2017).

China's severe air pollution, as a result of coal consumption, led China to diversified energy policies in renewables, natural gas and electricity. Following the reduction of emissions due to climate change targets set in the Paris Agreement, China became a key driver transferring CO_2 emissions and determining industrial OFDI with country-specifics to overcome environmental issues. Solar PV, wind and electricity infrastructures with new technologies of renewable energy are expected to reduce the costs and increase the energy appliances of households due to increasing urbanization by 2040. As an increasing domestic demand and diversification of outward energy investments, China has become an oil importer and exporter as well as technologies (IEA 2017). China's aim for the reduction of CO_2 emissions meets for climate action of Sustainable Development Goals (SDGs) as determinant of China's OFDI.

China has signed bilateral agreements with visa liberalization to establish economic zones carrying low-skill and medium-skill production operations out of country. Medium-skill production operations like industrial machinery, electronics, automotive components, medical devices constitute the flow of fourteen times larger than the low-skilled labor intensive productions each year. Therefore, the export business of standardized goods matters for creating value added production influencing economic growth (Moran, 2011b). China's greenfield investment as entry mode by the establishment of trade and economic zones is in industry, manufacturing, pipelines, real estate, renewable energy and communication sectors along the BRI especially in the Central and Eastern Europe and Africa, Gwadar-Pakistan, Morocco and also Myanmar. Low cost with qualified labor and young population enable Chinese companies' job creation and provide trade relations in addition to increasing export. In 2017, China established 99 economic zones accounting for USD 30.7 billion with 4364 enterprises creating 258000 jobs.

To materialize the BRI, China pursued geographical connectivity (Aybar, 2018). Although infrastructure industry constitutes long-term high risky payments in developing countries, other related industries like technology, production, transportation, ICT, oil, energy and digitalization brought new opportunities in international business. That's why the cooperation along BRI requires high policy to improve the relations between governments. Some of important projects -railway construction for 485 km combining Mombasa and Nairobi in Kenya financed US$ 14 billion in 2013, Line D pipeline from China to Turkmenistan with a cost of US$ 6.7 billion, Pupin Bridge in Belgrade-Serbia over Danube River and financed US$ 260 million as the first greenfield investment, a railway project starting at Piraeus Port in Athens-Greece to Belgrade over Macedonia, construction of Kingdom Tower tall of 1 km in Jeddah Saudi Arabia, US$ 225 billion valued mega infrastructure projects for city developments and for water & security due to 2022 FIFA World Cup in Qatar- have deepened countries' financial and economic relations.

Although Middle East (ME) region have high security risks over the average of world security, China and Iran signed to increase trade volume from US$ 50 billion to US$ 600 billion in ten years. Although ME has oil and natural gas rich lands, China's leadership of Solar PV investments create opportunity for nations gaining electricity from sunshine against climate change. After withdrawal from western markets, Russia's Gazprom and CNPC signed for 3 million cubic meters oil agreement purchased for US$ 55 million. In the midst of 2015, China and India made an agreement for trade valued US$ 22 billion and for transportation infrastructure valued US$ 83,6 billion. For China-Pakistan Economic Corridor investments were made in the fields of economic zone, renewable energy, power plants and transportation developments financed US$ 45 billion. The Southeast Asian countries, known as ASEAN, are the most important key partners of BRI and have signed 130 infrastructure contracts with China undermined US$ 250 billion (EIU, 2016). In services sectors such as leasing, finance, banking, technology, R&D, electricity and communications, China's outward investments increased from USD 26 367 million to USD 31 281 million (UNCTAD, 2017).

PATTERN OF CHINA'S OUTWARD FOREIGN DIRECT INVESTMENT

Previous empirical studies investigated China's OFDI from the perspective of Dunning's theories as OLI and IDP, IPI related to domestic income level. Until 2010, outward investments were insufficient due to China's poor domestic conditions and unequal income distribution through coastal and inland regions. Connectivity of geography through transportation, insufficient technology, reforms of government institutions and readjustment of domestic investments are some of the found challenges to drive China's OFDI effectively (Kun; Kuada and Sorenson, 2000; Buckley, 2004; Liu et al. 2005; Buckley et al. 2007; Gu and Han, 2013). The cultural difference, good management and qualified employees are some of the other challenges (Wang, 2015). Although China's OFDI has already been in academic interest, the BRI investments is a new subject and data is vague. The outward investment behaviors of Chinese multinational enterprises, as the manifestation of the drivers and motivations, effect the global economy in consequence of its traditional trade and policy (Burger and Karreman, 2010).

The European Union (EU) is the most important destination of China's OFDI. More than 40% of China's outward investments in developed countries goes to the EU, followed by different strategies in the Western and Eastern Europe. The fundamental macroeconomic conditions; market size and bilateral trade were found as the main determinants of China's OFDI in European countries due to good trade relations.

China's OFDI stock increased yearly on the average of more than USD 1 billion over the years between 2005-2012. After the 2008 global crisis, the investments of Chinese enterprises accelerated, especially in the UK and Germany in the fields of infrastructure, research and development (R&D), automotive, industrial machine, electronics and consumer products. China's OFDI in trade, logistics and distribution, business-related services such as banking, finance, insurance, and R&D went to Western Europe due to its high income level. The competitive labor force with high quality, lower cost ratio and low-income countries of the CEE influenced greenfield investment (GI) and merger and acquisition (M&A) entry. 90% of China's OFDI in manufacturing went to Central and Eastern Europe (CEE) especially Poland, Hungary and Bulgaria.

China's investments gradually created a developed investment climate for R&D, telecommunication technologies, clean energy and technological production in the CEE. Hungary, Italy, Greece, Portugal were found to be some of the Eastern European countries where China follows country specific strategy. Also, China's wealthy individuals invested their capital into real estate in Greece, Hungary, Latvia, Spain and especially Portugal. China's OFDI with the motivations of market seeking all over the EU, efficiency seeking in the Central and Eastern Europe, and strategic asset seeking such as brand management, know-how and technology, capital markets, R&D in Western Europe, is expected to create new business and trade, market and brands through bilateral agreements and flow of capital (Ying, 2014; Dreger et al., 2017).

Due to its diversified trade and production, China's OFDI is also motivated by natural resource seeking to supply its raw materials. Shanghai Baoshan Iron and Steel Corporation signed for Joint Ventures (JVs) in Australia, Brazil and South America. A distinguished article of Huseynov (2016) has empirically investigated the drivers of China's OFDI in infrastructure industry between the years 2005 to 2013, before the BRI. High deficit, strong institutions, large market size, national agglomeration, cultural proximity and free trade agreement were the strongest determinants, on the other hand geographical distance and macroeconomic stability were found the weak determinants of China's OFDI in host countries (Huseynov, 2016).

Another distinguished article is an empirical study explaining the impact of FDI on CO_2 emissions effect on China's going out strategy. The input-output of China's manufacturing has been increasing the carbon emission that is known as air pollution. It was defined by "carbon leakage" in The Kyoto Protocol in terms of the allowance of increase of emission in host country by taking over the production process from home country for the reduction of CO_2 emission in other words carbon trading system. Carbon constraint countries more likely intended to import from the nations with low environmental standards, in other words, providing advantage to non-constraint countries. Within the 34 host countries over the years 2000-2011, China's OFDI effected the industry selection related to the host country's technology level, energy structure in terms of coal, natural gas, oil, and production process. Hence, OFDI growth would lead to increases in CO2 emissions in the host countries. Mining and manufacturing industries are the drivers of China's OFDI due to air pollution (Ding et al., 2017).

The natural resources in Africa attracted China's capital through outward investments. Africa is an oil and extractive resource continent providing 1/3 of China's oil-supply and 40% of China's minerals and elements. China's OFDI with yearly increase of 46% over last decade improved trade relations and macroeconomic conditions pulling more Chinese OFDI into Africa. Also, China's exports impacting China's OFDI was related to market seeking motivations affected by GDP and GDP growth of host countries (Simon, 2015). Establishing Special Economic Zones (SEZs) in Africa was an important case, moving Chinese trade relations and export business forward. African policy and China's OFDI met export sectors. As a result of localization of Chinese production in Africa, China created the host nation's Rule of Origin (ROO), and China's OFDI was characterized by small and medium enterprises (SMEs) (Clarke, 2013).

The rising of Africa's working-age population in the opposite direction of China's aging population is complementarity and rapidly becomes the world's labor force (Dollar, 2016). Along the BRI Asia, the study on ASEAN region within the period of 2003-2014, natural resources and institutions were the profound determinants of China's OFDI for China's supply of raw materials for domestic production. Especially ASEAN and China FTA after Asia Financial Crisis further with an expansion through RCEP and cultural proximity have boosted China's OFDI. China's OFDI was also affected by the market size of host countries as GDP, GDP Per Capita and openness to trade (Anh and Hung, 2016). Also, there was a positive long-term impact of China's OFDI on its domestic investments. This is explained through country-specific effects in the multivariate analysis. In the meantime, investments from developing countries differ from the investments of developed countries because they face severe financial constraints (Ameer et al., 2017).

STRATEGIES OF CHINESE STATE-OWNED ENTERPRISES

The evolutionary transition of China's economy has been based on its historical governance and philosophy defining state-owned enterprises (SOEs) as the heartbeat of Chinese business system. The top-down dynamic governance forming complexity makes business environment vague, requiring further reforms and regulations of SOEs. The membership of WTO became the milestone of China for further reforms. The reforms of SOEs was meant not only rebuilding the organization but also the changes in logistics and distribution network (Child, 2003).

Agricultural modernization, increasing domestic consumption, industrial incentives, energy efficiency and environmental conservation, supply of human resources and technological innovation are some of the targeted 300 reforms in 25 fields adjusted by The National Development and Reform Commission (NDRC). Poverty alleviation, anti-corruption and ecological civilization for climate action constitute the main goals that are to be realized by 2035.

Outward investments of Chinese SOEs are managed by the government institution called SASAC, The State-Owned Assets Supervision and Administration Commission of the State Council carrying out the responsibility of ownership for investors as a shareholder. SASAC directs 110 non-financial central SOEs as corporate groups with their own extensive network of subsidiary companies. As of the end of 2014, there are 38 000 legal entities affiliated with the 110 central SOEs profiting USD 210 billion. The sectors are petroleum and petrochemical, metallurgical, machinery, mining, electronics, military, electricity, chemical, building materials, construction, geological exploration, communications and transportation, warehousing, telecommunications and trade (OECD, 2016). While MNEs run for 1% of the global economy, SOEs have major role dominating 10% of the global economy. SOEs have dominated Chinese economy and have been continuing to dominate its OFDI accounted for 84% with policy backed strategies in the new century (Goldsmith and Wagner, 2010).

According to the list of Forbes (2017) global 2000 companies, the top prior companies were heavily dominated by the Chinese SOEs in finance sector as ICBC with US$ 3,473 billion foreign assets, China Construction Bank with US$ 3,016.6 billion foreign assets, Agricultural Bank of China with US$ 2,816 billion foreign assets, Bank of China with US$ 2,611.5 billion foreign assets, Ping An Insurance Company with US$ 801 billion foreign assets, China Petroleum and Chemical with US$ 216.7 billion foreign assets, Bank of Communications with US$ 1,209.2 billion foreign assets, China Merchants Bank with US$ 855.1 billion foreign assets, China

Life Insurance with US$ 388.7 billion foreign assets, Postal Savings Bank of China with US$ 1,189.4 billion foreign assets, Industrial Bank with US$ 872.1 billion foreign assets, Shanghai Pudong Development with US$ 842.8 billion foreign assets, China State Construction Engineering with US$ 201.4 billion foreign assets, China Minsheng Banking with US$ 848.7 billion foreign assets, China CITIC Bank with US$ 853.5 billion foreign assets, Petro China with US$ 344.9 billion foreign assets (Forbes 2017), China National Offshore Oil Corporation with US$ 66 673 million foreign assets, China COSCO Shipping with US$ 43 076 million foreign assets, China Minmetals Corp. with US$ 35 156 million foreign assets, China State Construction Engineering Corp. with US$ 25 472 million foreign assets (UNCTAD, 2017).

Chinese firms with different entry mode of outward engagement to internationalize are explained below;

- **Joint Ventures (JVs)**

As the pioneering Chinese brand, Huawei has signed for JVs to make 3G handsets with NEC a Japanese IT enterprise and also cooperate with Microsoft to make networks for voice, data and video. Huawei has established R&D centers in India where happens to be a competitive market of ICT businesses and equipment competing with Cisco System (Wang, 2015). In 2016, USD 11.5 trillion digital economy for 15.5 % of global GDP is expected to increase to 24.3 % of GDP constituting USD 23 trillion of digitalized global economy by 2025. While digitalization impacts e-commerce, logistics, manufacturing, services trade and other ICT businesses, the average return of 1 USD investment to GDP will be 6.7 times higher for digital investments rather than non-digital investments. The Global Connectivity Index (GCI) evaluating the countries' engagement into digital economy shows the value of technology on a broader economic scale such as China's ranking 23 in 50 countries (Huawei, 2017). Huawei has 22% market share of mobile networks in the EU, Middle East and Africa.

- **The Wholly Owned Subsidiary**

China's OFDI going with subsidiaries is undertaken by establishing new entities in a foreign market. It aims to gain international brand awareness and management to enlarge overseas markets as ownership advantage. As the fourth largest white goods manufacturer, the Haier Group is one of the examples of implementing brand management strategy through trade, R&D and design centers for innovation. It has established 30 factories in different countries with a market share in the EU and US (Wang, 2015).

- **The Merger and Acquisitions (M&As)**

After Chinese firms started to internationalize with overseas investments to restructure their organizations through Initial Public Offering (IPO) in New York and Hong Kong Stock Exchanges with national companies as Petro China and Unicom, PICC, Air China, Bank of Communications, China Construction Bank, Shenhua Group, ICBC (OECD 2017), China's OFDI increased 44% from US$ 127 560 billion in 2015 to US$ 183 100 billion in 2016 due to M&A purchases of Chinese companies becoming the second largest investors (UNCTAD, 2017). In the new century, the top Chinese SOEs constituted in the fields of natural resources, oil and energy, transportation, construction, ICT and chemical metallurgy such as China National Petroleum Corp., China Petrochemical Corp., China National Offshore Oil Corp., CITIC group, Sinochem Corp., China Ocean Shipping Group, Aluminium Corporation of China, China Minmetals Corporation, China Poly Group, and privately held Zhejiang Geely Holding (Cui et al., 2016).

Chinese M&A provided entry for advanced technology, R&D and brand reputation to gain competitive assets such as Huawei, Lenovo Group and Nanjing Automobile. The main challenge to success is the management process in a foreign market regarding cultural differences and lack of qualified staff (Wang, 2015). In 2016, Shanghai Electric Power bought K-Electric for USD 1.8 billion through acquisition of a power generation and distribution company in Pakistan. China's largest electric company State Grid Corporation bought the largest Brazilian electric company CPFL Energia for USD 5.7 billion. China's oil company Sinopec purchased 33 % of US based Devon Energy in 2012 for USD 2.2 billion. China's petroleum company, CNPC, purchased 8% of Kaz Munai Gas National in 2013 for

USD 5.3 billion from Kazakhstan, which is an important destination for China and also Petroleos de Venezuela for USD 1.5 billion. The removal of sanctions in Saudi Arabia and Iran creates an investment climate for the benefit of China's OFDI along the BRI-Middle East region where Iraq grabs the attention of Chinese oil companies (EIU, China Going Global Investment Index, 2017).

Regarding the renewable energy sector, China has a competitive advantage as the driver of global relations for the cost advantage. China Three Gorges Corporation have the control of ten hydropower plants in Brazil. China Civil Engineering announced plans to build a hydropower plant in Nigeria. There are some other big projects in 2016-2017 like solar and wind power moving forward China's outward investments. China-Yingli company entered into Thailand with solar power manufacturing plant in 2016. Hydro China International invested to build a wind farm in Kazakhstan, and solar plants and four wind farms in Pakistan. In addition to energy issues, China is an investor of Nuclear Power and Reactors. In 2015, China General Nuclear declared to finance, construct and operate the Hinkley Paint C Nuclear Power Project in the UK. In 2017, China finished the construction of its fourth construction of nuclear power in Pakistan, and others continue in Turkey, Argentina and Romania.

Also, China expanded its M&A in the field of healthcare competing among the global market share with cost advantage in developing countries. China's Creat purchased a German blood plasma products maker, Biotest in 2017 for USD 1.5 billion, and Shanghai Fosun Pharmaceutical purchased a majority stake in an Indian drug company, Gland Pharma. Humanwell Healthcare purchased drug manufacturing in Ethiopia in the year of 2016 for USD 80 million. Artesun drug developed for Malaria in Africa was produced by the Chinese Fosun Pharma. In 2017, the biggest deal came from ChemChina SOE purchasing Syngenta, a Swiss chemical company for USD 43 billion. On the edge of developing finance technologies (fintech), Alibaba's Ali Pay and Tencent's WeChat Pay expand its mobile payment technologies in the Southeast Asia and EU, but not significant entry in overseas markets. Alibaba also generates e-commerce business through investments in the Southeast Asia and India (EIU, China Going Global Investment Index, 2017).

- **The Greenfield Investments (GIs)**

The first Chinese greenfield project of the BRI was Pupin Bridge in Belgrade-Serbia over Danube River and was financed US\$ 260 million. China's share of greenfield projects in the EU increased five folds from 2.9% to 15.4% through Chinese SOEs in 2016. Respectively France, UK, Finland, Greece, Germany, Poland and Netherlands were the destinations for China's greenfield investments in the sectors of real estate, renewable energy, electronics, automotive components, software and IT, financial services (European Political Strategy Centre, 2017).

China's total investment along the BRI valued USD 60 billion since 2013 while its outward investments totaled to USD 183 billion in 2017. According to MOFCOM Department of Outward Investments, 56 economic and trade zones has been established with a total investment of USD 18.55 billion. With a value of USD 50.69 billion, 1082 enterprises provided 177000 jobs with a tax payment to host countries USD 1.07 billion in 2016. An increase was observed from 12.1% to 18.3% in manufacturing with USD 31.06 billion, from 4.9% to 12% in software, and with USD 20.36 billion in information and technology in 2016. Haier Group cooperation with GE company was the most prominent one, driving China into global value chain. In 2017, China signed new agreements with 61 BRI countries worth USD 144.32 billion with an 14.5% increase to 54.4% and with a 30% turnover increase valued USD 85.53 billion. Leasing and commercial services, wholesale and retail industry, manufacturing and information transfer, software and IT totally were 74.4% rising fields of Chinese outward investments. A total of 341 M&A businesses in 49 countries in 2017 undertook 78% of outward investments valued USD 75 billion. Remarkably, 99 economic and trade zones accounting for USD 30.7 billion with 4364 enterprises in 44 host countries provided jobs for 258000 employees (MOFCOM 2017, 2018).

CONCLUSION

China's national modernization changed its economic policy by increasing wages and domestic demand, based on three main strategies: i) asymmetric investments to build its national security, ii) transition to services-trade economy, iii) FDI policies rebalancing the economy and reducing the currency reserve pressure on Yuan. China's Belt and Road Initiative, as a new phase for globalization, aims to build cooperation and connectivity among different geographies within 65 countries pursuing a diversified investment policy. Building a new geographical connectivity with SREB and MSR allows China to shorten the period of shipping through transportation and logistics with an expansion of new trade relations getting into global value chain.

Although the BRI data is not clear, the existing literature demonstrates that outward investments along the BRI are developing projects in infrastructure industry as economic zones, ports, bridges, railways, highways, airports through greenfield and M&A entry. Building a new geographical connectivity allows China to shorten the period of transportation and logistics on SREB and MSR with an expansion of new trade relations getting into global value chain and replace the domestic production with the transfer of technology and knowledge. China's multidimensional investment approach covers different needs of China's domestic economy. Therefore, China's OFDI pursue much more country specific rather than firm specific advantage with different motivations for natural resources, market seeking, efficiency seeking and strategic asset seeking in different continents. By the extension of these motivations, low-income and middle-income nations, cost advantage, market, national agglomeration, cultural proximity and free trade agreement to build trade relations are important determinants. Reducing carbon emission to contribute in the global climate change is also a new kind of determinant for China's OFDI. Real estate, construction, R&D, brand awareness, market share come forefront in high income and developed countries as the determinants of China's OFDI.

Even though natural resource companies still keep their importance, Chinese top SOEs are the main players in financial sector's access to RMB as fiat currency in international business. They aim to clench AIIB financing infrastructure investments and other BRI projects. Building economic zones with bilateral agreements shape Chinese manufacturing and cover new human resources. China's changing economic policy forms new mutual relations increasing interdependence. Consequently, China's multivariate and diversified investments along the BRI and non-BRI countries demonstrate that there will be long term impacts for home and host countries. Changing dimensions and reform policies of China will still be researched as long term issues in academic interest.

REFERENCES

[1] Ameer, W., Xu, H., & Alotaish, M. S. (2017). Outward Foreign Direct Investment and Domestic Investment: Evidence from China, *Economic Research, Taylor and Francis Online*.

[2] Anh, N. T., & Hung, D. Q. (2016). Chinese Outward Foreign Direct Investment: Is ASEAN A new Destination? *World Trade Institute*.

[3] Aybar S, (2018), Introduction, in Aybar (2018) et. al (Eds.), *China and the United States*, Cambridge Scholars Publishing, ISBN. 1-5275-0628-2.

[4] Buckley, P. J. (2004). The Role of China In the Global Strategy of Multinational Enterprises. *Journal of Chinese Economic and Business Studies, Taylor and Francis Online*.

[5] Buckley, P. j., Clegg, J., R.Cross, A., Liu, X., Voss, H., & Zheng, P. (2007). The Determinants of Chinese Outward Foreign Direct Investment. *Journal of International Business Studies, JSTOR*.

[6] Burger, M. J., & Karreman, B. (2010). Foreign Direct Investment, China and The World Economy. *Regional Studies, Taylor and Francis Online*.

[7] Child, J. (2003). China and International Business. In A. M. Rugman, & T. L. Brewer, *The Oxford Handbook of International Business* (pp. 681-715). NY: Oxford University Press.

[8] Clarke, N. (2013). Go Out and Manufacture: Policy Support for Chinese FDI in Africa. *Columbia FDI Perspective*.

[9] Cui, X., Shi, P., & Wang, W. (2016). *The Top 20 Chinese Multinationals: Changes and Continued Growth of Foreign Investment.* NY: Columbia Center on Sustainable Investment, Columbia University.

[10] Ding, T., Ning, Y., & Zhang, Y. (2017). The Contribution of China's Outward Foreign Direct Investment to The Reduction of Global CO_2 Emissions, *Sustainability*.

[11] Dollar, D. (2016). *China's Engagement with Africa From Natural Resources to Human Resources.* The Brookings Institute.

[12] Dreger, C., Schüler-Zhou, Y., & Schüller, M. (2017). Determinants of Chinese Direct Investments In The European Union, *Applied Economics, Routledge, Taylor and Francis Online.*

[13] EIU. (2017). *China Going global Investment Index.* The Economist Intelligence Unit.

[14] EIU. (2016). *One Belt One Road: An Economic Roadmap.* The Economist Intelligence Unit.

[15] *European Political Strategy Centre Issue 1: Greenfield Investment Monitor in Focus: China's Expansion in the EU.* (2017, May). Retrieved Fabruary 12, 2018, from European Commission: https://ec.europa.eu/epsc/sites/epsc/files/greenfield-investment-monitor-1.pdf

[16] FORBES. (2017). *GLOBAL 2000: The World's Biggest Public Companies.* www.forbes.com/global2000/list.

[17] Fung Business Intelligence (2016). The Belt and Road Initiative: 65 Countries and Beyond

[18] Goldsmith, S., & Wagner, D. (2010, 12 10). *Think Tank: The Rise of China as An Outward Investor.* Retrieved July 1, 2016, from FDI Intelligence: www.fdiintelligence.com

[19] Gu, X., & Han, L. Y. (2013). Empirical Research On The Rapid Growth of China's ODI: Based On Multinational Panel Data . *Applied Mechanics and Materials, Trans Tech Publications, Switzerland.*

[20] HKTDC. (2017, September 13). *The Belt and Road Initiative.* Retrieved November 20, 2017, from HKTDC Research: www.hktdc.com

[21] Huang, Y. (2017, July). *Why China Invests More in Europe Than In The US.* Retrieved January 20, 2018, from Financial Times: https://www.ft.com/content/a7641d16-6c66-11e7-b9c7-15af748b60d0

[22] Huang, Z. (2017, May 15). *Your Guide to Understand OBOR, China's New Silk Road Plan*. Retrieved January 20, 2018, from Quartz: https://qz.com/983460/obor-an-extremely-simple-guide-to-understanding-chinas-one-belt-one-road-forum-for-its-new-silk-road/

[23] Huawei. (2017). *Digital Spillover report*. Huawei Technologies.

[24] Huseynov, I. (2016). What Drives China's Outward Foreign Direct Investment in Infrastructure? *Victoria University of Wellington*.

[25] IEA. (2017). *World Energy Outlook, Executive Summary*, IEA Publications.

[26] Klasa, A. (2017). *The Africa Investment Report*. The Financial Times.

[27] Kuada, J., & Sorenson, O. J. (2000). Internationalization of Companies From Developing Countries. *Binghampton: International Business Press*.

[28] Kun, M. (n.d.). An Empirical Analysis on Chinese Outward FDI Development Path Based on IDP and IPI Models. *M&D Forum*.

[29] Liu, X., Buck, T., & Shu, C. (2005). Chinese Economic Development, The Next stage: Outward FDI? *International Business Review, 14*.

[30] MOFCOM. (2017, January 18). *Comments on China's Outward Foreign Direct Investment and Cooperation in 2016*. Retrieved January 30, 2018, from Ministry of Commerce People's Republic of China: http://english.mofcom.gov.cn/ article/newsrelease/policyreleasing/201701/20170102503092.shtml

[31] MOFCOM. (2018, January 18). *Comments on China's Outward Foreign Direct Investment in 2017*. Retrieved February 3, 2018, from Ministry of Commerce People's Republic of China: http://english.mofcom.gov.cn/article/newsrelease/policyreleasing/201801/20180102706193.shtml

[32] Moran, T. (2011b). Foreign Direct Investment and Development: Launching A Second Generation of Policy Research. Peterson Institute for International Economics.

[33] Moran, T. (2011a). *Foreign Direct Investment and Development: Launching a Second Generation of Policy Research, Avoiding the Mistakes of The First, and Reevaluating Policies for Developed and Developing Countries.* Washington DC: Peterson Institute for International Economics.

[34] Moran, T. (1999). *Foreign Direct Investment and Development: The New Policy Agenda for Developing Countries and Economies in Transition.* Washington DC: Peterson Institute for International Economics.

[35] OECD. (2017). *Economic Survey China.* OECD.

[36] OECD. (2016). *State-Owned Enterprises in Asia: National Practices for Performance Evaluation and Management.*

[37] Pioch, M. (2016). *BRICS In World Trade, Working Paper.* Retrieved January 9, 2017, from PRIMO, Power&Region In A Multipolar Order: http://www.primo-itn.eu/PRIMO/wp-content/uploads/2015/07/PIOCH-Working-Paper-3.pdf

[38] Simon, K. B. (2015). Key Determinants of China's Outward FDI to Africa. *Journal of Economics and Sustainable Development.*

[39] Tiezzi, S. (2015, May 9). *China's New Silk Road Vision Revealed.* Retrieved February 5, 2016, from The Diplomat: www.thediplomat.com

[40] UNCTAD. (2017). *World Investment Report.* www.unctad.org.

[41] Wang, Y. (2015). Outward Foreign Direct Investment of Chinese Enterprises: Review and Analysis. *Industrial Engineering and Management.*

[42] Xinhuanet. (2015). *Vision and Actions on Jointly Building Belt and Road.* Retrieved May 12, 2015, from Xinhuanet: http://news.xinhuanet.com/english/china/2015-03-28/c_134105858_2.htm

[43] Ying, F. (2014). An Analysis of China's Outward Foreign Direct Investment to the EU: Features and Problems. *International Journal of Management and Economics.*

GUIDELINES TO AUTHORS

Manuscript submission

Please send your manuscript submissions via electronic mail to the Florya Chronicles Editor, Prof. Dr. Sedat Aybar, at sedataybar@aydin.edu.tr. A cover letter with a statement of responsibility detailing what each author contributed to the manuscript should accompany the manuscript. An electronic mail will be sent to the corresponding author confirming receipt of the manuscript.

Editorial policy

Submissions to Florya Chronicles are rigorously refereed using a double-blind peer review process; authors and reviewers are anonymous to each other. Within a period of eight to ten weeks, the contributors will be informed about the reviewers' comments together with the decision of the editor about the manuscript as acceptance, minor revisions, major revisions or rejection.

Authors submitting manuscripts for publication in Florya Chronicles warrant that their manuscripts are the work solely of the author(s) stated, that they have not been previously published elsewhere nor are currently under consideration by any other publication and that the material contained within the work is not subject to any other copyright, unless required consents have been obtained.

Upon acceptance of an article for publication, all authors will be asked to sign an author disclosure form before the manuscript is scheduled for publication.

For all manuscripts reporting data from studies involving empirical research Florya Chronicles requires that the study have received formal review and approval by an appropriate institutional review board or ethics committee. This review and approval should be described in the manuscript's Methods section. Written informed consent from the participating subjects must be obtained.

All manuscripts must be submitted in English. Upon acceptance, language support for Turkish translation is given to those manuscripts submitted from abroad. An English-written version will be requested from Turkish authors if their manuscript is accepted for publication. Page proofs (as PDF files) will be sent by e-mail to the corresponding author, which has to be returned within five days.

Following publication the corresponding author will receive a copy of the Florya Chronicles issue containing the article, and a PDF file of the article via e-mail.

Please note that Florya Chronicles holds the copyright to all material it publishes. All accepted manuscripts and their accompanying illustrations may not be published elsewhere in full or in part, in print or electronically, without written permission from the Florya Chronicles. Any party seeking copies of material published in the Florya Chronicles must request permission.

Types of articles

Research Articles presenting ethical, original, critical, interdisciplinary, well-documented research with valid findings that add value to the existing knowledge, and with implications for policy are given preference.

Articles submitted as Case Studies are expected to have one of the following properties: cases challenging existing knowledge; novel technique, empirical or operative approach; management of social and private complications.

Reviews must include recent research and summarize important concepts. Use of diagrams, flow charts, tables and figures to enhance clarity rather than using block bulk of written information is encouraged.

Opinions should represent concise opinion pieces that address various topics of relevance to social sciences. These topics may highlight controversial opinions, or issues within the field. These topics may also include public sector management, mainstream and heterodox economics, management, government actions and policy, and commentaries on specific article or editorial that has been published by the Florya Chronicles.

Manuscript format

In preparation of their texts, the authors must pay attention to the points listed below:

Manuscripts should be prepared in A4 format with margins of 3cm from all the four sides. Pages must be numbered consecutively throughout the document. The entire manuscript should be typed in Times New Romans, 12 point font and half-spaced. Headings and subheadings should be typed in bold faced letters without a colon, or any other mark at the end. Headings should be typed in capitals while subheadings should be typed in lower-case, capitalize the first letter. Type all text justified margin. A blank line between paragraphs, between headings and text, and between references should be inserted, no indentation. The preferred submission format is Microsoft Word.

Manuscript sections

Order of manuscript should follow as Title Page; Abstract and Key Words (for Research Articles and Reviews); Main Text; Conflict of Interest; Acknowledgements (optional); References; Appendix/Appendices (optional); Tables; Figure Legends and should be combined into a single Word document.

Title Page: Each manuscript should have a title page providing the article title (in capital and bold faced letters and no more than 12 words); full names of each author with degrees, professional title; authors' institutional affiliations including city and country; name, address, telephone, fax and email address of the author responsible for correspondence.

Abstract and Keywords: No abstract is included in Opinions. Research Articles, Case Reports and Reviews should be accompanied by an abstract. The abstract should not exceed 250 words for Research Articles and 150 words for case Reports and Reviews. The abstracts should be in a structured format. Research Article abstracts should be under subheadings of Background, Objective, Methods, Results and Conclusion. Review articles should be structured as Background, Objective, Types of Studies Reviewed (a description of the types of studies reviewed), Results, and Practical Implications. Case Reports should have subheadings of Background, Objective, Case Description, and Practical Implications.

Keywords: (3-10 words) highlighting the article's most important topics should be listed afterwards.

Main Text: The main text of articles reporting Research Article should be presented in the order of Introduction, Methods, Results, and Discussion sections. The main text of manuscripts submitted as Research Articles should have a limit of 3000 words, those submitted as Reviews should have a limit of 5000 words. The manuscripts submitted as Opinions and Case Reports should be no more than 1500 words.

Conflict of interest: Please disclose whether any authors received any financial support for the conduct of the research or any commercial affiliations that could be considered to pose a conflict of interest regarding the submitted manuscript. If so, briefly describe the role of the sponsor(s).

Acknowledgements: If applicable, acknowledgements should be grouped in a paragraph at the end of the text and before the references. Permission and approval of the wording must be obtained from the person thanked.

Tables and Figures: A maximum of four figures and four tables may be submitted. Tables and figures must be numbered consecutively. Ensure that each table and figure is cited in the text. Tables should contain information on Table number and a brief and explanatory title. Do not draw vertical rules in tables. Figures should be submitted separately in TIFF, JPEG or EPS format in grayscale. Figures should have a caption. Citations: Cite references in the text with regard to APA style[1]. In APA style, footnotes are not used to cite sources. Instead, you provide the authors' last names and publication dates within the body of your paper. Here are some examples.

1. One work by one author.
Example: Leary (2008) argued that...
Example: ...self-motives are actually interpersonal motives (Leary, 2008).

---

[1] APA citation style information is directly taken from the document prepared by Prof. Borton for Hamilton College, Department of Psychology.
http://www.hamilton.edu/documents/Citing%20Sources%20APA%20Style.pdf last accessed on 03.06.2015.

2. Quoting directly . Example: When you think of the long and gloomy history of man, you will find more hideous crimes have been committed in the name of obedience than have ever been committed in the name of rebellion" (Snow, 1961, p. 24).

References: All references cited in the text must be included in the list of references at the end of the paper. The accuracy of references is the responsibility of the author. References are listed in the order in which they are cited in the text. A maximum of 30 references for Research Articles, 50 references for Reviews and 10 references for Opinions and Case Reports should be included.

Examples of References:

1. Journal article
Horberg, E. J., & Chen, S. (2010). Significant others and contingencies of self-worth: Activation and consequences of relationship-specific contingencies of self-worth. *Journal of Personality and Social Psychology,* 98, 77 – 91. doi: 10.1037/a0016428.

2. Article or chapter in an edited book
Chang-Schneider, C., & Swann, W. B. The role of uncertainty in self-evaluative processes: Another look at the cognitive-affective crossfire. In R. M. Arkin, K. C. Oleson & P. J. Carroll (Eds.), *Handbook of the uncertain self* (pp. 216-231). New York, NY: Psychology Press.

3. Entire authored book
Gilovich, T., Keltner, D., & Nisbett, R. E. (2011). *Social psychology* (2nd ed.). New York: W. W. Norton.

4. Entire edited book
Vohs, K. D., & Baumeister, R. F. (Eds.). 2011. *Handbook of self-regulation: Research, theory, and applications*. New York, NY: Guilford.

For more information on APA citation style:
http://www.apastyle.org

Printed in February 2019
by Rotomail Italia S.p.A., Vignate (MI) - Italy